How to Draw & Paint Cars

Tony Gardiner

First published in February 2008 by Veloce Publishing Limited, 33 Trinity Street, Dorchester DT1 1TT, England. Fax 01305 268864/e-mail info@veloce.co.uk/web www.veloce.co.uk or www.velocebooks.com.
ISBN: 978-1-84584-124-9/UPC: 6-36847-04124-3

Readers with ideas for automotive books, or books on other transport or related hobby subjects, are invited to write to the editorial director of Veloce Publishing at the above address.
British Library Cataloguing in Publication Data - A catalogue record for this book is available from the British Library. Typesetting, design and page make-up all by Veloce Publishing Ltd on Apple Mac.
Printed in India by Replika Press.

How to Draw & Paint Cars

Tony Gardiner

VELOCE PUBLISHING
THE PUBLISHER OF FINE AUTOMOTIVE BOOKS

Contents

TONY GARDINER

Foreword & Acknowledgements

From the moment that early motorcars trundled down the dust-covered roads of Europe, owners of these newfangled contraptions known by the populace as 'horseless carriages', challenged fellow automobilists to races with 'I wager mine is faster than yours' taunts. Thus, many challenging races took place, with artists of that period depicting the scenes of these heroic early contests.

The motorcar evolved quickly from an initial top speed of barely 10mph before 1904 to purpose-built racers stripped down to minimal bodywork, with huge engines capable of speeds of 60mph, all piloted by intrepid drivers and very brave riding mechanics.

As motor racing developed, artists captivated by this new phenomena recorded on paper and canvas, and in a variety of mediums, the titanic struggles of these early racing machines. These cars, like today's Formula One vehicles, had only one function: to race.

Most artists who create images of cars competing in motorsport are generally enthusiasts themselves, and so may gravitate towards venues where some kind of motorsport is taking place. It is at the lesser events, i.e. club meetings, where access to the competing cars is easier and you can view them at close hand, thus finding plenty of material for your sketchbook and some on-the-spot drawings, using pencils or charcoal (you could make watercolour sketches but only in the early stages). Carry the minimum materials, and remember to take a camera to record details you might easily miss and for future reference when creating a painting from your sketches back in your own home or studio. For want of a better

Tony Gardiner

5

World Champion
Oil painting on canvas board.

Mike Hawthorn, driving for Enzo Ferrari, became
Britain's first World Champion driver in 1958.
This oil painting depicts Hawthorn's Ferrari 246 Dino
ahead of Juan Manuel Fangio in the Maserati 250F, and
Hawthorn's team mate, Peter Collins, in another Ferrari
246, during the 1958 German GP at the Nürburgring.

'The Ring' is set in the heavily-wooded Eifel Mountains
of Germany, so the menacing conifer forest created a
dark green backdrop, and contrasts with the bright red
Ferrari and its blue nose cone.
The technique for oil paintings is very similar to that
of acrylics, except that oils dry much more slowly, but
the advantage of this is that mistakes can be rectified
quickly if needed, unlike watercolour, where you are
committed to getting it right first time!

explanation 'drawing live on location' teaches the importance of observation, which is the basis of creating convincing, visual images, utilising basic skills in perspective and tonal values.

My personal preference is for attending pre-race practice days or sessions when there are fewer people about, which allows the artists to mingle in the paddock area and use the skills required to be a successful automobile artist.

Another venue sometimes available is a friendly local garage or car restoration business, which specialises in vintage or classic cars and might give you access to its workshops. More and more today we are governed by 'Health & Safety' rules, which mean that some establishments won't allow access to these areas, which is sad, because, as a student, I spent many hours in such workshops, sketching everything from Ferraris to little vintage Austin Sevens.

Depicting the racing car is no different from any other motorcar you care to mention, and within the pages of this section I give encouragement and some practical advice on the rules of drawing and painting, avoiding certain pitfalls, becoming more observant, and fine-tuning your artistic skills. The best way to achieve all of this is to practice, practice, practice, coupled with determination and desire to become a successful artist at drawing and painting the motorcar in all shapes and forms, from whatever period in automobile history over the last one hundred and twenty years.

Author's note:

I do not suggest for one minute that this book is the key to being able to instantly draw and paint cars; there is no quick-fix and only experience will achieve this. You will find only a few step-by-step guides within these pages, with many examples of rough working drawings and sketches, plus finished paintings in various mediums, together with a caption describing how I achieved the end result.

Over time you will develop your own distinct methods of working, so my sole objective is to awaken your creativity and interest in painting cars, plus, give you a kick-start to what lies ahead.

At various times within the text I mention particular brands of artists' materials – paints, brushes, pencils, etc. These are my personal preferences and in no way intended to influence your choice of materials.

The ultimate challenge for artists of all abilities is to create images that will not only provide personal pleasure and satisfaction, but possibly even fame and fortune in the years ahead.

Acknowledgements

I am greatly indebted to Pat Heddon for typing the manuscript, Philip Young for his support and encouragement over the years, and to the many individuals and companies whose commissions are reproduced in this book. Lastly, to Stacey Grove at Veloce Publishing for accommodating my every whim and foible.

Introduction

When Carl Frederich Benz's first experimental two-stroke engine burst into life in January 1879, I wonder if he realised quite what he had unleashed upon this planet, changing it forever. From that day on, mankind has conducted a love-hate relationship with the internal combustion engine and the horseless carriage, which, over the past one hundred and thirty-plus years, has revolutionised travel and communication.

The automobile also captured the imagination of contemporary artists, who mostly portrayed this newfangled horseless contraption as ridiculous, compared with real horsepower. This attitude gradually changed as vehicles became more reliable and accepted, along with the advent of the first motor races that were taking place across Europe. Two of the most famous held on open public roads were the Paris-Bordeaux-Paris event held in 1895, and the great intercity race of Paris-Vienna in 1902. These were quickly followed by many more such races, including the early Grand Prix held on closed public roads. By this period, artists were portraying the awesome spectacle of these monster racing machines piloted by heroic drivers and their riding mechanics, locked in feats of epic proportions and endurance with wheel-to-wheel duels that, tragically, sometimes resulted

1895 – Frederick Lanchester built England's first successful motorcar.

1907 Rolls-Royce Silver Ghost – the
world's first luxury motorcar.

in fatalities amongst spectators and competitors alike.

Two French artists of this period captured the scenes and atmosphere of these early races. Rene Vincent was one; trained as an architect, he created images of fast-moving automobiles with all the correct details, plus his knowledge of perspective gave his illustrations great depth. The other was Ernest Montaut, who created speed and movement within his paintings by leaving out the spokes on wheels, including speed lines, and fading away the rear end of the portrayed vehicle. Some of his work graced both inside and outside (in a series of ceramic tiled panels) walls of the Michelin building in London.

British artists quickly took up the challenge of creating images of the automobile explosion

1914 Model T Ford – the first
mass-produced motorcar.

1929 Bentley Speed Six – won the Le Mans 24 hour race in the same year.

on society, the greatest being Gordon Crosby and Bryan de Grineau. Both of these artists enthralled readers of motoring magazines of the period such as *Autocar*, *Motor* and *Car*, their illustrations bringing to life all the drama and action of the previous week's motor races across the continent of Europe, and here in Great Britain.

In America, the most well-known artist depicting the motoring scene was Peter Helck, although, in his early days, he could best be described as an industrial artist. By 1912, he was illustrating motor racing scenes for companies such as Veedol Oil and Champion Spark Plugs, and in posters for Revived Vanderbilt Cup Races of 1936 at the Roosevelt Speedway. Helck's first real break came in the mid-1940s when he was commissioned to create a series of colour spreads of motor racing scenes for the magazine, *Esquire*.

At the end of World War II, motorsport enthusiasts in Europe were eagerly awaiting the restart of motor racing with cars that had been saved from destruction by being hidden, walled up and stored in barns, sheds and cellars during six years of conflict. These were wheeled out to once

Buick 2-door Electra 1959 – the last year of the big tail fins on American automobiles.

1972 Lamborghini Countach
– supercar of the 1970s.

1979 Porsche 930 Turbo – a
German masterpiece.

again do battle on the motor racing circuits of Europe.

Along with the motorsport enthusiasts came new artists, some of the best known of this post-war period being Roy Nockolds, Frank Wootton and Terence Cuneo. All produced magnificent oil paintings over the decades depicting automobiles and other transport subjects such as aircraft and locomotives. Other equally well-known artists included Gordon Horner, whose wash sketches reproduced in sepia tint within the pages of

Autocar were a feature of this motoring magazine for many years.

In the early 1960s, a new artist, Michael Turner, arrived on the scene, with dynamic pencil sketches of motor racing action, followed by the now-familiar guache paintings that are known worldwide. Michael's early works first appeared within the pages of that other main British motoring publication of the time, *Motor*. Another 1960s artist who became well-known during this and following decades was Dexter Brown, whose

1985 Audio Quattro – the most significant car of that decade and beyond.

distinctive style of vibrant colours, mixed with broken and refracted light images, appeared on posters and race programmes.

America, during the early 1950s, experienced an upsurge in European-style road racing, with the creation of many circuits such as Watkins Glen in New York State, and the West Coast circuits of Pebble Beach, Laguna Seca Raceway and Riverside, among others, alongside more traditional style oval speedways such as the famous 'Brickyard' in Indianapolis. To race these road circuits, wealthy Californians imported European sports cars – Ferraris, Maseratis, Jaguars, Aston Martins, Porsches, Morgans and MGs – to race alongside Corvettes, Thunderbirds and, later, Scarabs, Mustangs and Cobras.

The two most popular magazines to report all of this racing action were *Road & Track* and *Car & Driver*, which employed many more artists and illustrators than did the motoring press in the United Kingdom. William A Motta – art editor of *Road & Track* between 1971-1983, produced dynamic paintings and fostered the use of other equally exciting freelance artists within the pages of *Road & Track*, including the German-born genius, Walter Gotschke, with his loose-style watercolour paintings, Richard Corson, and Ken Dallison with their unique pen and ink with colour wash drawings,

Toby Nippel, creator of detailed classic car profiles, and the vivid and vibrant painting of Hector Luis Bergandi, while John Berkey created imaginary present and future motor scenes. These are just a few of the artists whose work has graced the pages of *Road & Track* in particular, and the American motoring scene in general, over the past sixty years.

Let us also not forget the many technical illustrators on both sides of the Atlantic over the years, whose cutaway illustrations have, literally, given us an inside view of the workings of automobiles. Guy Lipscombe, Max Millar, L W Cresswell, Vic Berris, Theo Page, James Allington, Brian Hatton, David Kimble, Vittorio Del Basso and Tony Matthews have all created everything from line and wash drawings, to ink and full colour illustrations.

Another of motoring art's disciplines which often gets forgotten is the cartoon. In this sphere, two stand out from the rest in the author's opinion. Russell Brockbank's mastery and knowledge of the automobile, mated to a brilliant sense of humour, is unsurpassed, along with the character he created: motoring buffoon 'Major Upsett'. In America, it is Stan Mott who catches the imagination with the antics of the 'Cyclops' Racing team.

It is only now, at the beginning of the 21st century, that motoring art is at long last being recognised by the art world for its merits, and judged alongside the works of other contemporary artists for its portrayal of modern times.

Therefore, within the pages of this publication, I will not 'try to teach my grandmother to suck eggs' but will present an insight to drawing and painting cars for complete beginner and accomplished artist alike. By combining observation and dedication with technique, all will be able to create pleasing and professional results.

I would like to feel that this book will appeal to all lovers of automobiles, and that, from any age, they will be able to draw inspiration from its pages.

Angus Shields, 9 years-old, created the drawings below of one of his favourite cars – the Maserati Quattroporte – conveying his idea for a concept car powered by a 560cc engine (Jaws), and his version of a Tuk Tuk. From little acorns! Well, who knows, one day, perhaps ...

There is no shortcut or special formula to teaching art in any form, but, through the pages of this book, I will endeavour to guide, inform and assist the willing student through any hazard on the long and winding road ahead.

Tony Gardiner
West Sussex
England

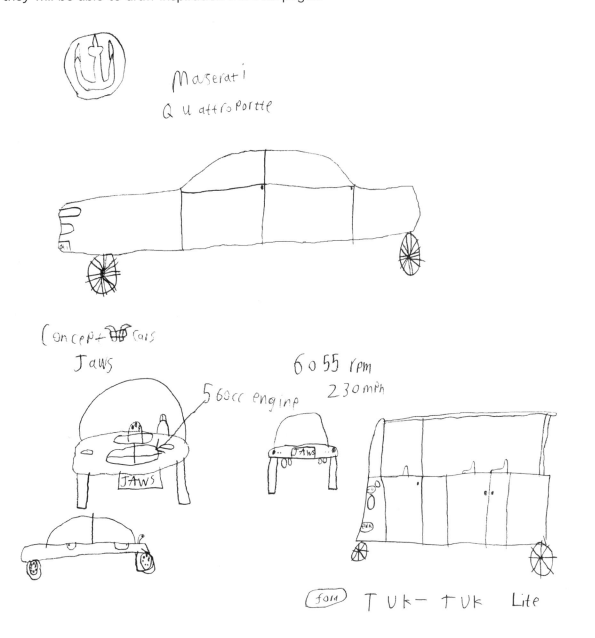

Principles of automobile motion

Most pictorial representations of motorcars generally depict them in motion both on and off the track. With this in mind, I have decided to devote this first chapter to precisely that subject, but will only briefly outline the principles which apply. Talk of drag coefficients and aerodynamics won't really mean that much to the artist; what is important is for the student of automobile art to understand, especially with racing cars, is that aerodynamics increase a car's performance by helping it go faster and stick to the road like glue when cornering, etc.

Three aerodynamic forces act on an automobile: Drag, Lift and Side Force, combined with parallel forces acting on three axis – X, Y and Z – as well as the moments rotating round these axis: X = Roll (Mr); Y = Pitch (Mp) and Z = Yaw (My).

I am not saying for one moment that to become successful as an automobile artist you have to understand vehicle aerodynamics, but it does help to understand, to a certain degree, how and why various cars act in different ways when in motion.

The two most obvious forces which could influence how the artist portrays an automobile in motion is pitch and roll. If you are portraying cars at speed, especially Formula One or Group C sports cars, they will pitch back around their Y axis (see fig 4). This pitching moment is related to the angle of attack of the wind over the car's nose, or if you are depicting a car cornering hard, the side forces come into play showing roll around the X axis.

Aerodynamics, of course, play a major role in the design of modern Grand Prix cars: as well as the all-too-familiar rear wing, we now have bargeboards, winglets, diffusers, aero flaps and chimneys; the list is endless because of the

Car wants to rotate around offside front wheel

Rear wheels losing adhesion allowing the back end to 'hang out'

Opposite lock applied to correct oversteer

Direction of car travel

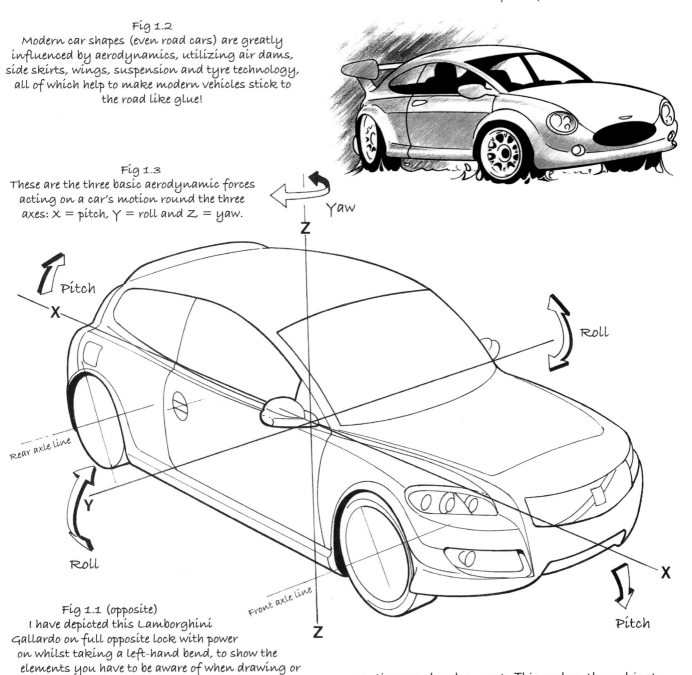

Fig 1.2
Modern car shapes (even road cars) are greatly influenced by aerodynamics, utilizing air dams, side skirts, wings, suspension and tyre technology, all of which help to make modern vehicles stick to the road like glue!

Fig 1.3
These are the three basic aerodynamic forces acting on a car's motion round the three axes: X = pitch, Y = roll and Z = yaw.

Yaw

Z

Pitch

X

Roll

Rear axle line

Y

Roll

Front axle line

X

Pitch

Z

Fig 1.1 (opposite)
I have depicted this Lamborghini Gallardo on full opposite lock with power on whilst taking a left-hand bend, to show the elements you have to be aware of when drawing or painting a car in this situation.

(1) Current sports cars have very little body roll, hence they maintain a 'flat' appearance.
(2) The driver has applied opposite lock to help bring the car back to its intended direction.
(3) The back wheels have lost adhesion, hence the back end of the car 'hangs out' – this creates a spectacular image for the artist.

For this particular pencil drawing I have used a series of soft pencils ranging from HB to 4B, a blender and a soft eraser.

continuous development. This makes the subject interesting but any motoring artist will have to be aware of detail changes, literally from race-to-race.

To a certain degree, the same applies to current road vehicles as manufacturers make subtle model changes year-to-year whereas, say, forty years ago a model might be in production for five years with no noticeable change. Even racing cars changed very little from year-to-year, and certainly not in the prolific way of current racing cars.

The average man in the street can spot new models as they appear, but the motoring world

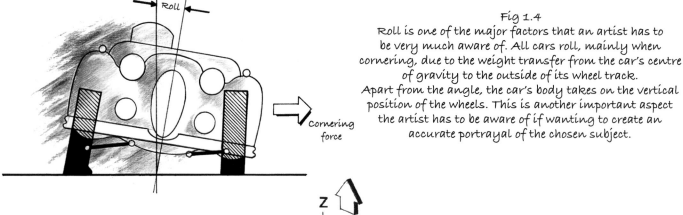

Fig 1.4

Roll is one of the major factors that an artist has to be very much aware of. All cars roll, mainly when cornering, due to the weight transfer from the car's centre of gravity to the outside of its wheel track.

Apart from the angle, the car's body takes on the vertical position of the wheels. This is another important aspect the artist has to be aware of if wanting to create an accurate portrayal of the chosen subject.

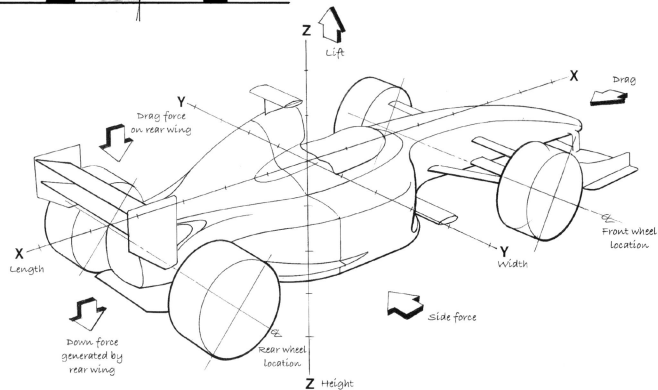

changed in the early 1980s when models such as Ford's Sierra arrived on the scene. Cars like the Sierra – nicknamed the 'jelly mould' by the press – began a revolution in automobile shape and design, heralding a new era of soft, organic shapes which, to an extent, is still with us today. Suddenly, sales pitches included drag coefficient details (soft, slippery shapes improved airflow, hence there was less drag and better fuel consumption).

I hope this brief introduction to the world of automobile aerodynamics will help the student to understand why cars look the way they do, and the dynamics of the way they perform.

Fig 1.5

I am not going to pretend I understand aerodynamic forces and moments on automobiles, nor that it is necessary for an artist to do so, but to know the basics of aerodynamics and the effect on automobile behaviour does assist understanding what we see when a car is in action.

Components of aerodynamic force acting on the three axes X, Y and Z are drag, lift and side force (see fig 1.5); a further three rotate round these axes: yaw, pitch and roll (see fig 1.3). It is the latter three which we can see in action the most, although yaw is really only experienced from behind the wheel. We can see that pitch really comes into play under braking; i.e. the nose comes down (or dips) and the tail goes up. Roll is caused mainly when cornering – modern cars have very little roll owing to much stiffer suspension and better built-in anti-roll devices. However, take a car built any time during the period 1950-1980 and most will roll like a small ship in a storm (see fig 1.8).

These two illustrations show something a car is not intended do: fly ... aeroplanes do that!
In theory, it is the suspension designer's job to keep all four wheels firmly attached to terra firma so that the car maintains adhesion, drive and steering at all times. However, under certain conditions with full power on over short humps, cars do leave the ground.
In these paintings I have tried to show two examples from different eras of how the artist can depict this phenomena.

Fig 1.6
This is an ink line drawing with a watercolour wash drawn on line & wash board. The subject is a 1966 Mini Cooper 'S' with all four wheels off the ground. When this does occur, the suspension drops to its maximum extension because it is no longer supporting the car's all-up weight.

Fig 1.7
The technical aspect of this drawing is that of the previous fig but I have used a mixture of mediums to create this drawing, including pastel pencil, markers and watercolour drawn on 'Buttercup' Daler Canford paper, as the yellow was virtually the same tone as the SEAT WRC I was portraying.
To give the impression of the car leaving the ground, I use diagonal lines going in the direction of the car's forward movement, as this helps to catapult the car into the air.

Figs 1.8 (right) & 1.9 (below)
What I am showing with these two drawings (fig 1.8, a 1960 Jaguar 3.8 saloon and fig 1.9, a 2006 Bugatti Veyron), is the amount of body roll that these cars from different decades take on when cornering.
The sixties Jaguar, although set up for racing with stiffer suspension and anti-roll bars, still has quite a significant degree of 'roll angle', mainly due to a high CG (centre of gravity) and bodyweight.
Today's Bugatti Veyron benefits from the technology that has improved all vehicles with better suspension and the use of lightweight materials. Hence, the reason why today's motorcars have very little body roll.
For the artist, knowing how to depict a car in action within its correct historical periods and how it performed, is quite important.

fig 1.10
Radicals Racing
Watercolour, 56cm x 76cm/20 x 30in
Courtesy of David Redwood

When drawing and painting current sports racing, be aware that racing cars such as these are designed with very little ground clearance, and exhibit minimal body roll (see fig 1.4).
At times this doesn't help the artist, but painting a dark shadow underneath the vehicle helps to accentuate the car's colour and shape (see fig 7.1).
I find that creating lighter tones on the road surface close to the subject and very dark tones for the shadow can overcome the problem.

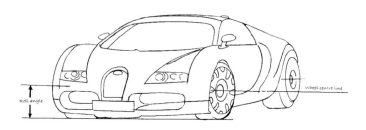

② Basic drawing construction

efore embarking on the first steps of car illustration, students should have at least some knowledge of the basic principles of vehicle construction, although generally this is acquired over time and with experience of working as an artist/illustrator. Passing on my experience could prove beneficial to those students who are interested in portraying the motorcar, either for pleasure or in a professional capacity.

The car has evolved over the last one hundred-odd years, with early versions having the same terminology as the horse-drawn carriage; i.e. the dashboard is known today as the I/P or instrument panel. The dashboard was literally just that; a board to stop stones thrown up by the horse's hooves dashing the coachman and his passengers in the face. Another example is where driver and

Fig 2.1 (bottom)
I have included this basic line drawing of a typical current 2-door saloon car, showing its exterior body panels and other components. Why? You might well ask! I firmly believe that if you know what you are looking at and are able to understand the basic breakdown of a car's exterior components, then you are well on the way to being able to create accurate representations of any vehicle you wish to name.
Far more components go towards making up a car's bodyshell, but these are the only ones I think you will really need to know about.

Note:
*Tumblehome is the measured angle from a vertical line, taken at the car's waistline, of the amount the side glass area leans in toward the car's centre line. This greatly affects the reflection created on the glass caused by the curvature of the surface area.

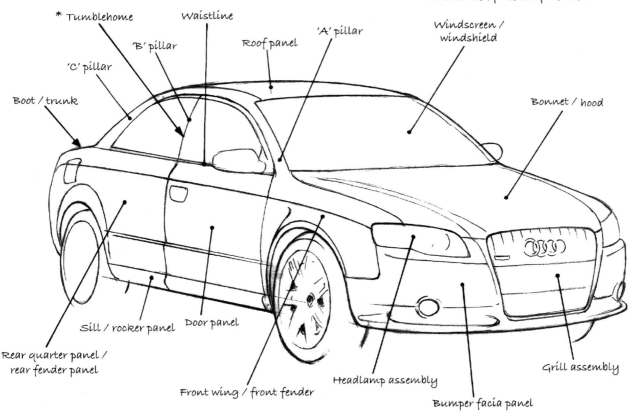

* Tumblehome • Waistline • 'A' pillar • Windscreen / windshield • B' pillar • Roof panel • 'C' pillar • Boot / trunk • Bonnet / hood • Rear quarter panel / rear fender panel • Sill / rocker panel • Door panel • Front wing / front fender • Headlamp assembly • Bumper facia panel • Grill assembly

Fig 2.1 (right) & Fig 2.1/1
(below)
Alfa Romeo 147
Canford paper (Guardsman
Red)
28 x 17cm/11 x 17in
Pencil, marker & pastel

First I boxed up a chosen view (see fig 2.1/1 below), roughly drawing in height, length and width, plus wheel centre lines, etc. Then, using photographic references from press release photos, I created a rough sketch which, on completing to my satisfaction, I transferred onto the Canford paper using that to give the car's colour.

I always choose to block in all the dark areas first, in this case, using a black Magic Marker, working the rest with a range of graphite pencils from 2B to 7B, and finally using white pastel for the highlights. Again, because I created this sketch depicting the car in motion, I tended to let the rear end fade away slightly.

A final note: because marker pens have a tendency to bleed through this type of paper, do not leave anything you want to keep under the drawing whilst laying down the marker pen.

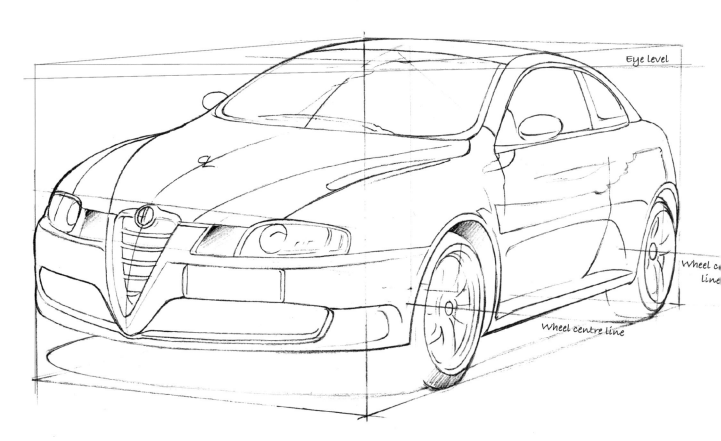

Eye level

Wheel c
line

Wheel centre line

Fig 2.3
To show you can create a drawing with virtually anything, this sketch of a 1959 Austin-Healey Sprite – a small, popular sports car of that period – shown with its bonnet raised, was drawn while I was still a student at art college.

It was actually drawn in the workshop of a local garage whilst this car was in for a service. Likewise, to practice your drawing skills, why not try something similar, or even draw a family of cars parked in the street?

As I mentioned previously, our ancestors used very basic tools. Similarly, this ink sketch was created with a sharpened stick dipped into non-waterproof writing ink, whilst the wash shading was created by smudging the sketch by dipping a finger into the ink and water. You can draw with anything and with very little outlay in materials.

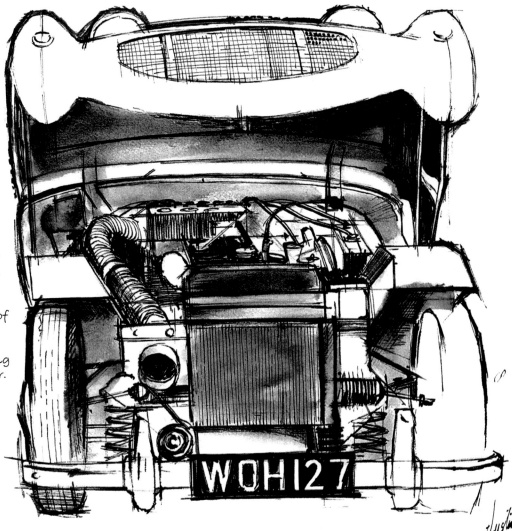

Fig 2.4
When creating any image of a car in motion it will have a driver, and maybe a passenger.

It is important to get the correct proportions between car and occupants. I have chosen to illustrate this point by using a diagram of Ford's famous 1960s sports GT, the GT40, so called after its overall height of 40 inches. What this shows is a known measurement; 40 inches, on the average human, is roughly to the hip joint. Another helpful statistic is that the human head will fit 7.5 times into the body. So many times I've seen paintings

with heads so small that body height 'A' would make a GT40 look like a people carrier; likewise 'C' would make it go-kart size with the driver's feet poking out of the grille.

'B' is the correct proportion so, as previously mentioned, check where your figure's hip joint falls in relation to the car's height and you won't go far wrong.

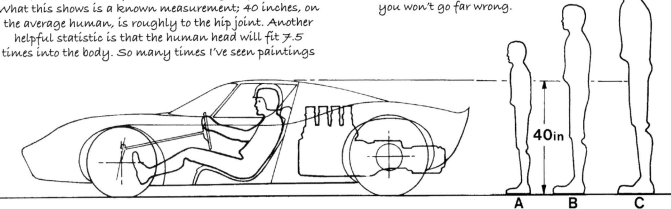

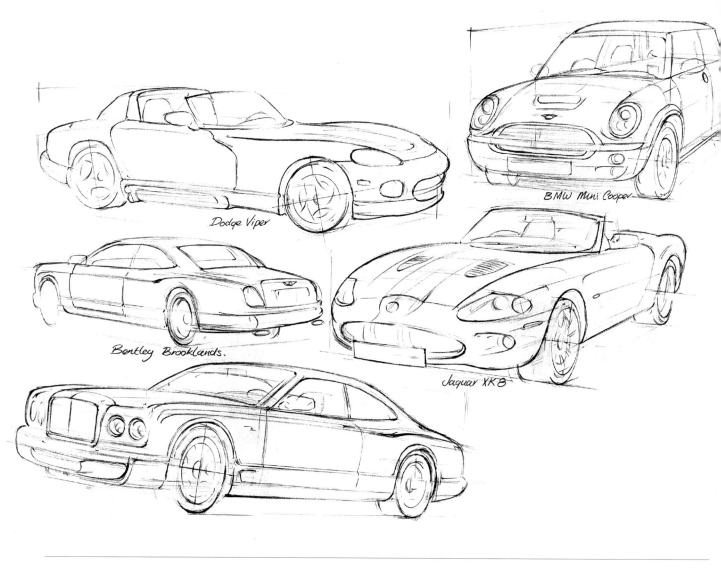

Dodge Viper

BMW Mini Cooper.

Bentley Brooklands.

Jaguar XK8

front passenger place their feet, the splash panel, still used in current car construction. Again, in coaching days, this was intended to protect the occupants of the coach from being covered in mud and water.

Once you know the basic principles of car construction, you are able to construct your drawing safe in the knowledge of what and why helps create the particular shape of the motorcar you are depicting. Initially, the motorcar appears to be a very complex shape but the trick is to visualise it as a basic rectangular box, roughly the proportion of a shoe box. Whether you are using a perspective grid or drawing your vehicle freehand, create a box in the perspective angle you wish to draw, and mark out the basic lines; the obvious ones being roof and waist lines. Once you have established these, everything else generally falls into place. Next, you can mark out the major features; i.e. wheel centre lines, wheelarches, headlamps, grilles, etc, at which point it might also be advisable, if you are going to include the human

Fig 2.5
At this stage you should have some idea of the basics of constructing a car drawing, so my suggestion is to practice by sketching various models, from luxury saloons, sports car, and 4x4s to basic models. Try to select different angles and not worry about detail at this stage, instead concentrating on proportions and wheel ellipses.
The more you sketch, the easier you will find it becomes to achieve the correct proportions without having to think twice about it.

Fig 2.6
Brighton National Speed Trials

This selection of pencil sketches was first drawn in lightly whilst at the actual event, then enhanced later from photos taken for reference.

The GT40 replica was caught when queuing to line up for the start, so it was moving every few minutes. Go with it; the car doesn't change, you can fill in the background later.

The other three – the Austin Seven Special, AC Cobra replica and the Bentley Special – were parked in the paddock, so I had a longer period to work on these sketches.

For this exercise I use a Pental Sharplet 0.5 retractable pencil with an HB or B lead. It is more convenient than having to sharpen a conventional pencil when 'going live'.

figure in your painting, either in or standing by the car, just to rough them in to get the proportion right (more about this later).

Wheels, for obvious reasons, are a very important feature, so it's important to get the location of the centre lines and wheel size correct and to the right proportion. The trend with current models is for much larger wheels set at each corner. This revolution in wheel layout was brought about in 1959 by the introduction of the original Mini created by Sir Alex Issigonis. Until then, most cars had large bodywork overhang at the front and rear. As you begin to build up the car's features, run perspective lines through your rough sketch as it helps keep it all in proportion, both front to rear and side to side, and helps line

continued page 28

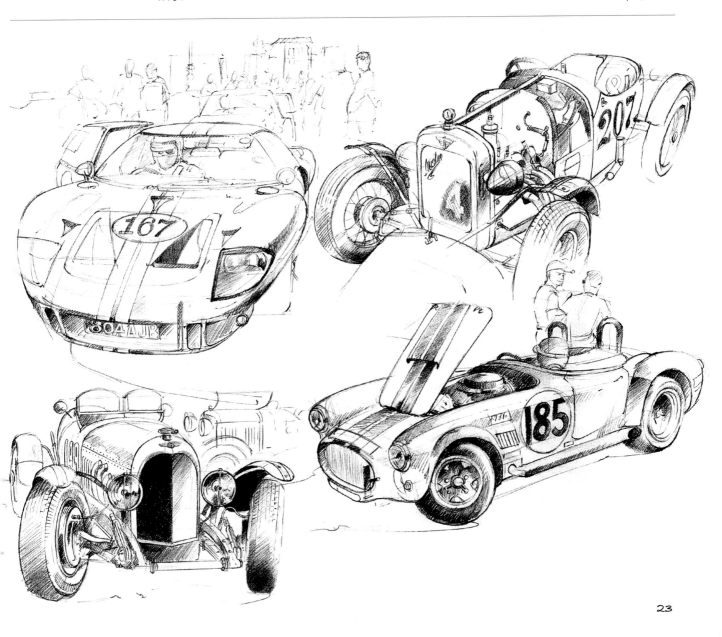

Fig 2.8 (below)
Another workshop pencil sketch, this time a famous
sports car from the 1950s, the Italian-built Lancia
D24. It was this model, driven by Alberto Ascari, which
claimed victory in the 1954 Mille Miglia.
It's workshop scenes like this that make interesting
compositions in their own right, and this car was in
for a major transmission overhaul with its wheels off
and front suspension dismantled. Remember, under a
car's bodyshell there are a host of components, so try to
understand as much as possible about how it works.
This sketch was drawn in an A3 wire-bound 90gm
sketchbook using soft pencils; i.e. B
and 2B, plus a 4B for
emphasising darker
shaded areas.

Fig 2.7 (opposite)
These workshop scenes present ideal opportunities for real-life sketches. The workshop was that of a motor racing school which used a variety of cars, from single-seaters through to high-performance vehicles such as a Ferrari 308, Lamborghini Countach, Porsche 911, Jaguar E Type, AC Cobra, and a selection of classic sixties sports cars.

All of these make excellent subjects, especially if they are undergoing maintenance – the Porsche Carrera 911 was having a major brake overhaul, whilst the Renault single-seater racing car was getting its electrics looked over.

Take every opportunity you can to try your drawing skills in such environments, as it is excellent practice to create paintings from the actual object and not just photographs, as happens in a lot of cases.

The actual sketch was drawn on Bockingford 140gm watercolour paper, using 4B and 2B pencils. Due to the surface texture of the paper, the sketch has a rough, spontaneous look.

Fig 2.9
Caterham Seven – watercolour sketch
Courtesy of Neil Worsfold

Here is a basic watercolour sketch created 'live'. The main object of this exercise is to practice drawing and painting cars from life.

The Caterham Seven is one of Britain's best-known kit cars, and a direct descendant of the world-famous Lotus Seven designed and built by Colin Chapman. As such, it is a good example of basic automobile engineering, and an excellent choice of subject to hone the skills needed to become a car artist.

For a sketch of this nature, I suggest you concentrate on getting an image down on paper. Do not worry too much about correct ellipse angles, or even accurate perspective; as long as it looks right, all these aspects can be corrected later.

Once again, I used a sheet of 190gm Bockingford tinted watercolour paper, using colours from the inexpensive Windsor & Newton 'Cotman' range; a wash of Paynes Grey and Phthalo Blue was used for the background and the car's aluminium body panels. Sepia, Burnt Sienna and Yellow Ochre were used for brickwork, floor, etc, plus details. To pick out the car's nose cone, wings, etc, permanent white designers' gouache was used because of its density.

You could choose almost any car for this exercise, although you do need something with a bit of character.

Fig 2.10 & Fig 2.10/1 (inset)
This quick watercolour rough sketch was produced using photographs as references for obvious reasons.
The subject is a Mercedes-Benz 300 SLR which, despite its very battered appearance, was driven to victory on the 1955 Targa Florio by Stirling Moss and Peter Collins. I chose to portray Stirling Moss driving the car at high speed, despite its damaged front end.
First, I produced a quick line ink drawing using a conventional pen for a sharp outline, then laid in a pale colour wash over this. To achieve the silver paint finish in which all Mercedes competition cars were painted, I used a washed-out Ultramarine Blue with odd dabs of Daveys Grey. The background and road surface are a mixture of the usual Burnt Sienna, Raw Umber, Yellow Ochre and Lamp Black.
Unlike the Caterham Seven sketch (see fig 2.9), this was drawn on 200gm white Cartridge paper. If you use this type and weight of paper unstretched, or if it is still a page in a sketchbook, do not make it too wet as it will crinkle quite badly.

up door pillars, etc, on the side furthest away from you. This is why I think a basic knowledge of car construction helps to understand what can be seen from certain viewpoints; those which are out of sight are generally symmetrical from side to side, so it is important to line everything up to achieve a correct image.

Above all, the correct prespective is imperative, otherwise the entire exercise is a waste of time. Most of us use only two-point perspective because most cars have not got enough height to worry about using three-point where you have converging verticals, unless you are drawing a double-decker bus or a huge, intercontinental truck from a high viewpoint.

The last point I would like to make within this section is: remember to treat the car as a whole object not a series of bits stuck together. Don't get carried away with working on the headlamps and ignore the body shape round them, or any other part; get the overall appearance correct and it will all fall naturally into place.

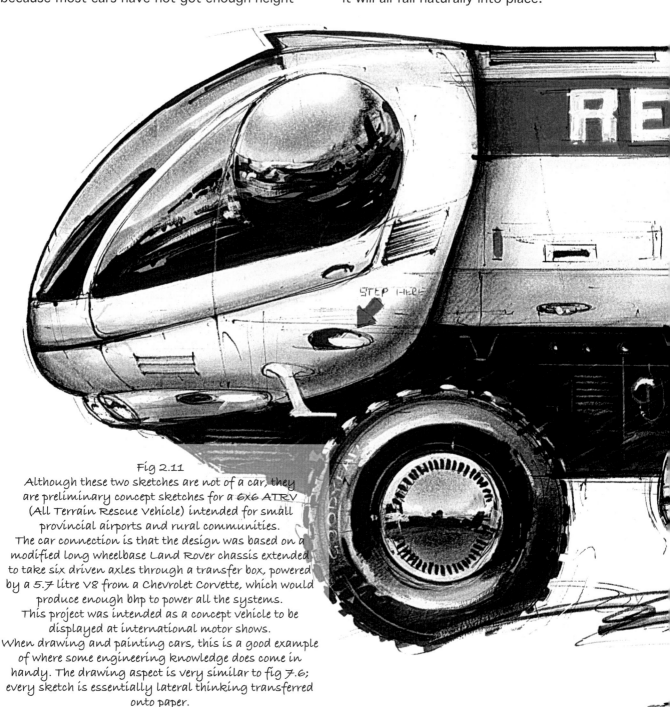

STEP HERE
RE

Fig 2.11
Although these two sketches are not of a car, they are preliminary concept sketches for a 6x6 ATRV (All Terrain Rescue Vehicle) intended for small provincial airports and rural communities.
The car connection is that the design was based on a modified long wheelbase Land Rover chassis extended to take six driven axles through a transfer box, powered by a 5.7 litre V8 from a Chevrolet Corvette, which would produce enough bhp to power all the systems.
This project was intended as a concept vehicle to be displayed at international motor shows.
When drawing and painting cars, this is a good example of where some engineering knowledge does come in handy. The drawing aspect is very similar to fig 7.6; every sketch is essentially lateral thinking transferred onto paper.

③ Perspective

ossibly the most important ingredient of any painting, sketch or technical illustration is perspective, sometimes referred to as 'the art of recession'. Generally, for drawing cars in a composition, only two-point perspective is required, but if a large, highly-detailed illustration is the object of the exercise, then three-point is necessary. This can be achieved – especially if the illustration is commissioned commercially, when time and money is of the essence – by using a perspective grid (see fig 3.2). There is, of course,

Fig 3.1
Porsche 935 cutaway
CS10 paper
56 x 76cm/20 x 30in

The inspiration for this cutaway drawing was a large-scale plastic kit, which was built by a friend who always enhanced his models with incredible extra details. He kept a photo diary of the build process, so it was from these references that I constructed this ink drawing cutaway – really, just for the pure enjoyment and challenge.
The previous year I had paid my first visit to spectate at the Le Mans 24hr race, where a particular Porsche 935 variant was raced and entered by Martini Racing.
I enlarged my friend's photographs of the build process in order to draw in all the details piece-by-piece, laying in perspective by eye.
The initial drawing was created on detail paper then transferred to the Frisk CS 10 paper (this is the surface of the normal CS 10 board), from which the ink drawing was finally created.

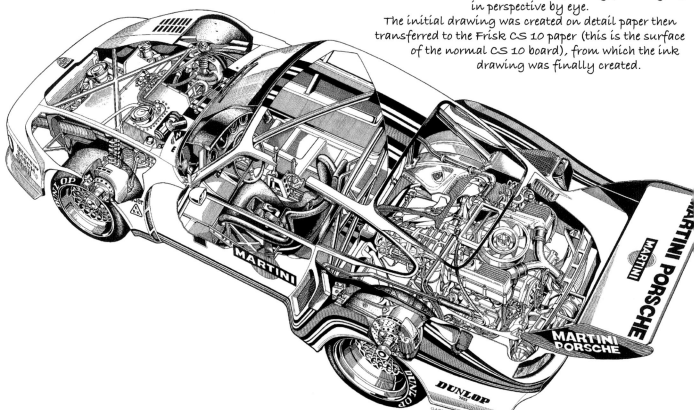

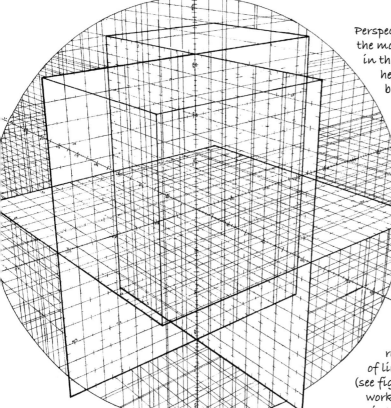

Fig 3.2
Perspective grids come in various layouts, but probably the most used – certainly by me throughout my career in the aircraft and auto industries – is that illustrated here. This layout of the grid helps speed up the first basic principles of creating technical illustrations. First, it gives you the datum lines; i.e. the X, Y and Z plots to work from (see fig 3.2/1 overleaf).

This establishes the overall dimensions: X = length, Y = width and Z = height. When these have been established, you can create your basic outline in the true scale and proportion of your chosen subject, working from either works drawings (computer or manual) and photographs, or the actual vehicle. Most pictorial images from computer design programmes are generated in isometric; i.e. all lines intersect at an angle of 30 degrees (see fig 3.2/2, below left). I have worked with this system within the auto industry but found that working with a true perspective grid to be the most satisfying and rewarding. With isometric you have to use weight of line to give depth and recession to your illustration (see fig 3.2/3 below). Shown overleaf is an initial rough working drawing in pencil created using isometric projections from a design engineer's computer, with the generated imaging of a typical 1990s 4-door family saloon car.

However, illustrators do cheat. You can to a certain extent redraw isometric off a CAD system by adjusting the projections into perspective.

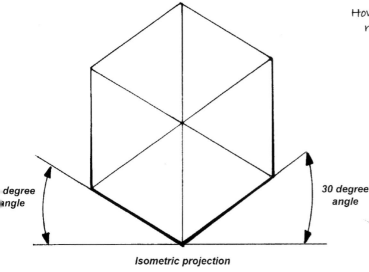

degree
angle   30 degree
                                          angle

Isometric projection

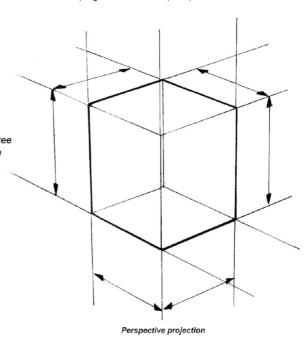

Perspective projection

Fig 3.2/2 (above) and 3.2/3 (right)
All projected lines in isometric projection remain parallel to each other, which seems to make the drawing distorted because the lines do not recede to converge on each other. The horizontal lines drawn at right angles to each other are all at 30 degrees to the horizontal. All verticals remain vertical, whereas lines drawn in perspective, both horizontal and vertical, eventually converge to an unseen vanishing point (See fig 3.2/3).

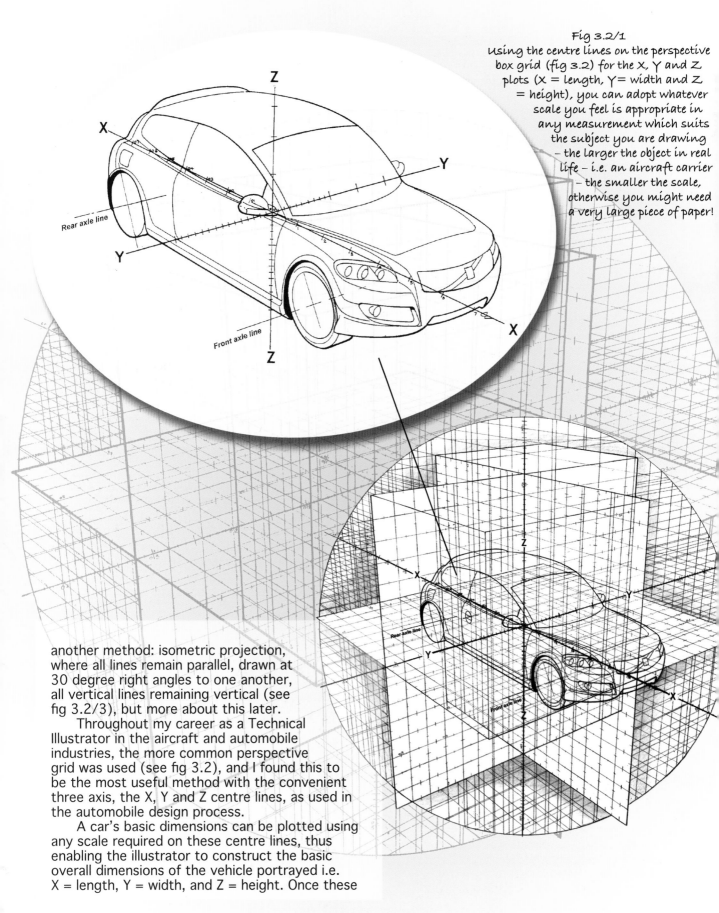

Using the centre lines on the perspective box grid (fig 3.2) for the X, Y and Z plots (X = length, Y= width and Z = height), you can adopt whatever scale you feel is appropriate in any measurement which suits the subject you are drawing – the larger the object in real life – i.e. an aircraft carrier – the smaller the scale, otherwise you might need a very large piece of paper!

another method: isometric projection, where all lines remain parallel, drawn at 30 degree right angles to one another, all vertical lines remaining vertical (see fig 3.2/3), but more about this later.

Throughout my career as a Technical Illustrator in the aircraft and automobile industries, the more common perspective grid was used (see fig 3.2), and I found this to be the most useful method with the convenient three axis, the X, Y and Z centre lines, as used in the automobile design process.

A car's basic dimensions can be plotted using any scale required on these centre lines, thus enabling the illustrator to construct the basic overall dimensions of the vehicle portrayed i.e. X = length, Y = width, and Z = height. Once these

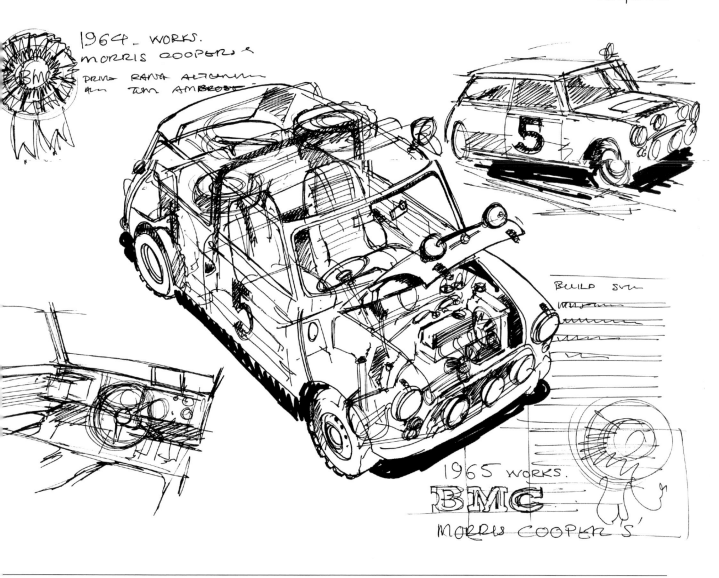

1964 - WORKS.
MORRIS COOPER S
DRIVER RAUNO ALTONEN
Co TIM AMBROSE

BUILD SVL
WILLIAMS

1965 WORKS.
BMC
MORRIS COOPER 'S'

dimensions have been established, more detailed dimensions – such as the waistline, door shut lines, windscreen depth, position of headlamps, etc – can be added until the entire outline is correctly drawn (see fig 3.2/1).

Once this has been established and the intention is to produce a scale-accurate drawing or a cutaway illustration, a whole new set of dimensions come into the equation. Firstly, you need to establish the basic components within your car's outline: engine, transmission and final drive, i.e. front wheel, rear wheel or 4x4; secondly, steering and suspension and, lastly, interior layout, seats, door trim, instrument panel, centre console, etc, plus all the other components that go into a car's construction such as radiator, air con system, battery, electrics, fuel and brake lines, fuel tank, exhaust, wheels, tyres, and spare wheel location.

Fig 3.3/1
This is my first layout sketch for fig 3.3 on what was virtually a piece of scrap paper. From this sketch gradually evolved the final artwork. In many cases, not much of the original concept ends up in the final artwork ... but you have to start somewhere!

Gremlin will always try to ruin your painting by rushing you; take your time and think ahead!

Fig 3.3/2.
To acquire this information, I contacted owners and motor museums, attended classic car rallies and anywhere else I knew these cars would be appearing.

It would be the same process if you were drawing something more exotic, like a Ferrari GTO. Most owners of interesting cars are quite willing for their cars to be photographed for such projects.

One of the main problems with this type of illustration is deciding just what components to depict and which to leave out. Remember, whatever angle you choose, look at the nearest components and gradually cut back the layers, choosing the most important parts.

Try a simple exercise: first draw a basic outline of any car you have access to and draw the engine detail by cutting away the bonnet/hood. Then, draw the interior, cutting away the roof and doors and, perhaps, removing the front wheel so you can see the suspension.

Once you feel happy with this simple exercise, produce a more complicated drawing from a different angle, and add more internal detail.

Some artists make a living out of producing only this type of illustration.

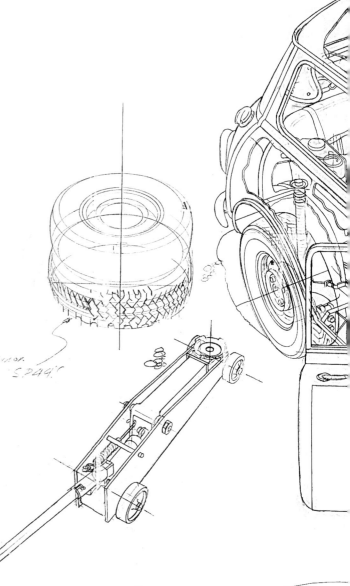

SMALL ILLUSTRATION
1½ HRS. TUESDAY.

MON: 23
10-30am—
12-45—
1-30pm
4-00pm

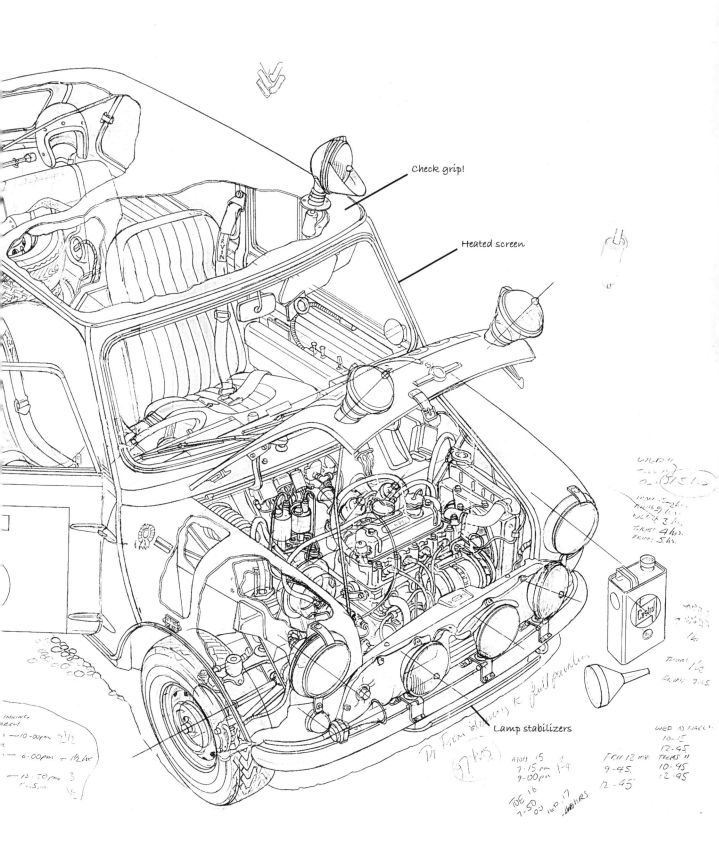

Check grip!

Heated screen

Lamp stabilizers

Fig 3.3
Mini Cooper 'S'. Winner of the 1965 RAC International
Rally of Great Britain
Ink/gouache

This cutaway illustration was created as a centre spread
in a book.
This was drawn from an enlarged photograph of a Mini
Cooper, taken at the angle shown. I traced the basic
outline and external details, then added all of the extra
detail using photographs taken from other similar
'Works' Minis, as this particular car no longer existed.

All of these components should be included within the overall illustration, but, perhaps due to the angle of projection, some might be hidden by others, so a choice has to be made of which is the more important. This is where some knowledge of car construction comes into play because, through experience, you will know what to include, leave out, or half-show by ghosting; showing the item hidden behind another (see fig 3.4).

When you have completed the initial drawing this must be transferred onto the surface for the finished illustration. I use a simple method of creating my own sheet of carbon by scraping, say, the lead from a 4B pencil and spreading it onto a

continued page 43

Fig 3.3/2a-d
These four photographs are typical of the reference
material I find useful when constructing technical
cutaway illustrations.
For this particular drawing, I used thirty photos
depicting everything from minor details like badges
and door handles, through to engine, suspension, seats,
tyres, trolley jacks, and even the tool bag on the back
seat.

(a) Main spot/fog lamp brackets
(b) Lucas 5 inch back-mounted fog lamps
(c) Special pattern rally seats, driver/navigator
(d) Engine bay: engine, brake seno, alternator,
carburettors, etc

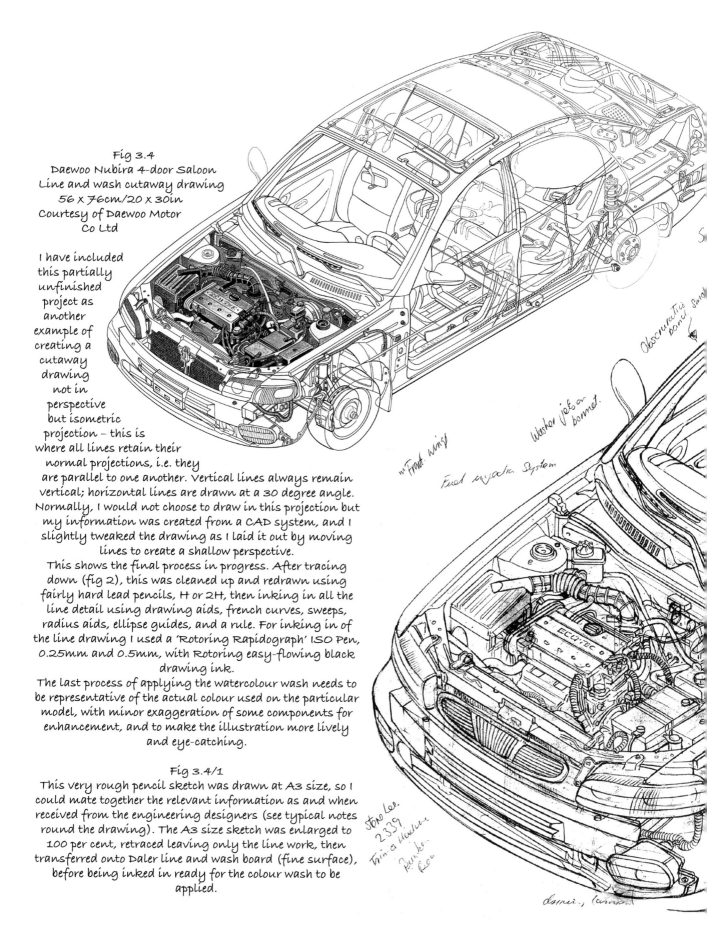

Fig 3.4
Daewoo Nubira 4-door Saloon
Line and wash cutaway drawing
56 x 76cm/20 x 30in
Courtesy of Daewoo Motor
Co Ltd

I have included
this partially
unfinished
project as
another
example of
creating a
cutaway
drawing
not in
perspective
but isometric
projection – this is
where all lines retain their
normal projections, i.e. they
are parallel to one another. Vertical lines always remain
vertical; horizontal lines are drawn at a 30 degree angle.
Normally, I would not choose to draw in this projection but
my information was created from a CAD system, and I
slightly tweaked the drawing as I laid it out by moving
lines to create a shallow perspective.
This shows the final process in progress. After tracing
down (fig 2), this was cleaned up and redrawn using
fairly hard lead pencils, H or 2H, then inking in all the
line detail using drawing aids, french curves, sweeps,
radius aids, ellipse guides, and a rule. For inking in of
the line drawing I used a 'Rotoring Rapidograph' ISO Pen,
0.25mm and 0.5mm, with Rotoring easy-flowing black
drawing ink.
The last process of applying the watercolour wash needs to
be representative of the actual colour used on the particular
model, with minor exaggeration of some components for
enhancement, and to make the illustration more lively
and eye-catching.

Fig 3.4/1
This very rough pencil sketch was drawn at A3 size, so I
could mate together the relevant information as and when
received from the engineering designers (see typical notes
round the drawing). The A3 size sketch was enlarged to
100 per cent, retraced leaving only the line work, then
transferred onto Daler line and wash board (fine surface),
before being inked in ready for the colour wash to be
applied.

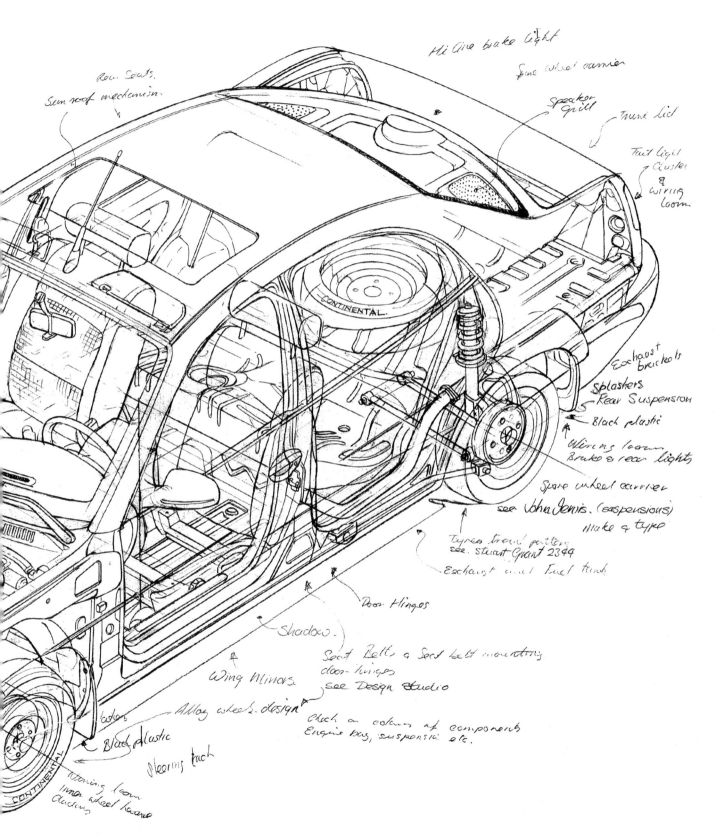

Hi line brake light

Spare wheel carrier

Speaker Grill

Trunc lid

Rear Seats.

Sun roof mechanism.

Tail light Cluster & wiring loom

Exhaust brackets

Splashers Rear Suspension

Black plastic

Wiring loom, Brake & rear lights

Spare wheel carrier

see John Jenis. (suspensions)

make & type

Tyres tread pattern see. Stuart Grant 2349

Exhaust and Fuel tank

Door Hinges

Shadow.

Seat Belts & Seat belt mountings

door hinges

see Design Studio

Wing Mirrors

Alloy wheels. design

Check on colours of components Engine bay, suspension etc.

Black plastic

Splashers

Steering rack

Wiring loom inner wheel house Clucting

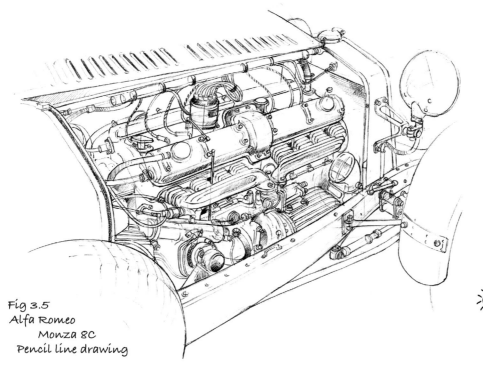

Fig 3.5
Alfa Romeo
Monza 8C
Pencil line drawing

DIRECTION OF SUNLIGHT

Technical illustrations can be created in many guises, to
either provide instructional information or as a pleasing
pictorial representation of the internal workings. This pencil
line drawing is an example of one way to create such an
illustration.

Select an interesting model of your choice (preferably the
actual car) and make a fairly accurate sketch, working
out the proportions by eye – this helps improve your visual
interpretation of what you actually see, whereas other
illustrations in this chapter have been created using
photographs and engineering drawings taken from
computer-generated design systems.

This pencil line drawing falls somewhere in the middle. I
drew this vintage Alfa Romeo engine bay because I found
its engineering very appealing, and it's a beautiful piece of
design.

Fig 3.6
Pencil drawing
London street scene

Here is an example of a full working pencil drawing depicting
a typical London street scene of the late 1950s, from which a
scaled-up version can be turned into a painting.

If, for any reason, you have no immediate plans to complete a painting,
as in this example, it is advisable to add notes if there are areas of
concern which need more research, or colours you might need to know
about at a later date.

'Life', unfortunately for the motoring artist, is not all about fast cars
and glamorous motor racing circuits. You should be able to portray
any subject asked of you with the same amount of dedication and
professionalism as with more glamorous subjects.

I deliberately chose to create this drawing on 190gm 'Bockingford' tinted
watercolour paper, and used the complete range of lead pencils from
2B–8B in the 'Mars Lumograph 100' series, plus the odd dab of titanium
white watercolour.

TRAFALGAR SQUARE

CHURCH SPIRE OF
ST MARTIN-IN-THE-FIELDS

SOUTH AFRICA HOUSE
LIGHT GREY STONE

CHECK! TYPE OF LANTERN

CHECK! BUS ROUTE
HEAD CODES.

NEED MORE DETAIL
OF THE CHERUBS

BLACK

FORDSON VAN.

ROLLS ROYCE SILVER WRAITH
by PARK WARD: COLOUR BLACK & GREY.
(might need making slightly larger.)

41

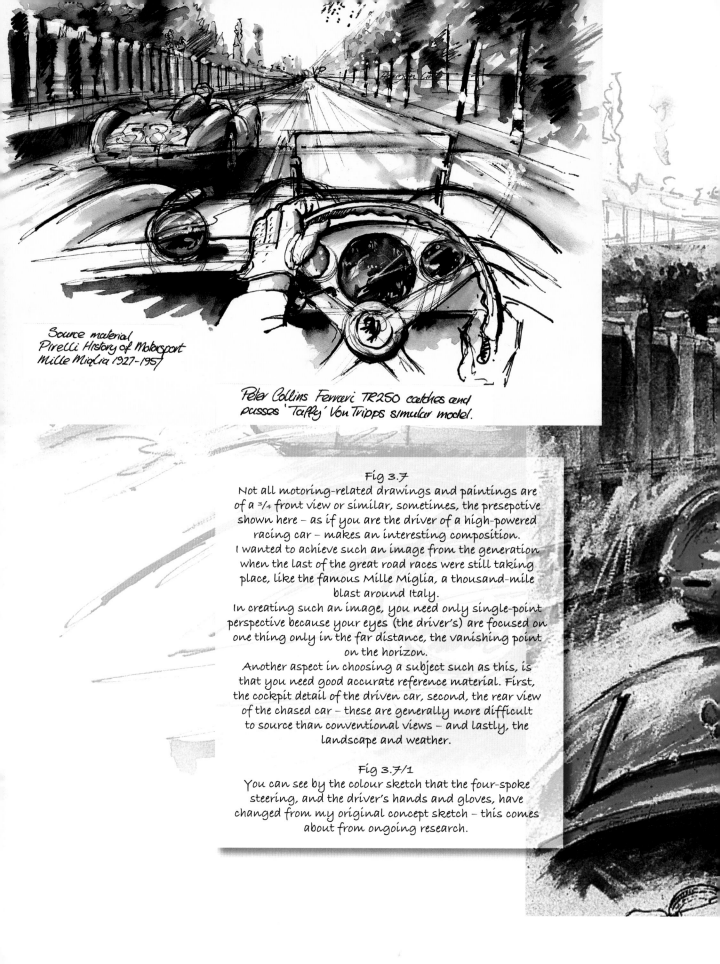

Source material
Pirelli History of Motorsport
Mille Miglia 1927-1957

Peter Collins Ferrari TR250 catches and
passes 'Taffy' Von Tripps similar model.

Fig 3.7
Not all motoring-related drawings and paintings are
of a ¾ front view or similar, sometimes, the presepctive
shown here – as if you are the driver of a high-powered
racing car – makes an interesting composition.
I wanted to achieve such an image from the generation
when the last of the great road races were still taking
place, like the famous Mille Miglia, a thousand-mile
blast around Italy.
In creating such an image, you need only single-point
perspective because your eyes (the driver's) are focused on
one thing only in the far distance, the vanishing point
on the horizon.
Another aspect in choosing a subject such as this, is
that you need good accurate reference material. First,
the cockpit detail of the driven car, second, the rear view
of the chased car – these are generally more difficult
to source than conventional views – and lastly, the
landscape and weather.

Fig 3.7/1
You can see by the colour sketch that the four-spoke
steering, and the driver's hands and gloves, have
changed from my original concept sketch – this comes
about from ongoing research.

sheet of tracing paper with a soft cloth or cotton wool, then tracing over the working drawing. Then, either lightly redraw in pencil or begin to ink in the lines, or you might just want to create a full colour illustration, using different hues to emphasise various components, and light and shadow to create depth: the choice is yours!

Fig 3.8
Photo references

I cannot stress enough that a comprehensive photographic reference archive is essential. I can assure you that, as an artist, you will always be searching for detail and accuracy, and not only for exotic cars, past and present, but also for everyday road cars: where else will you find details of a 2005 Ford Focus or a Swatch car? My philosophy is: "If it moves, take a photo, if not, still take a photo"! Towns, landscapes, skies ... you never know when you are going to need such reference material.
As in the motto of the worldwide Boy Scout movement 'Be prepared'.
This is a selection from my archive showing everything from street scenes to car details.

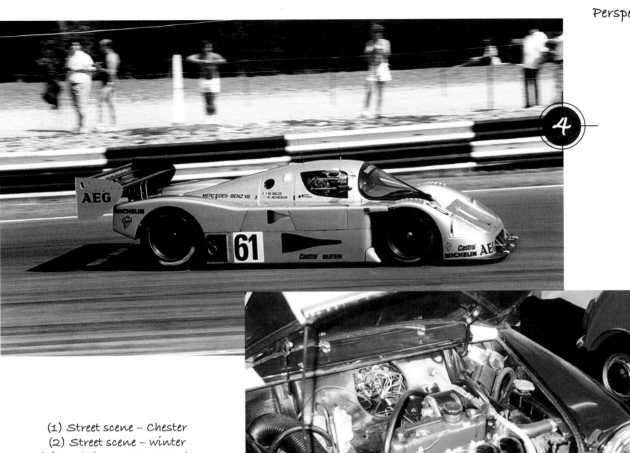

(1) Street scene – Chester
(2) Street scene – Winter
(3) Backdrop – Monte Carlo
(4) Mercedes-Benz C9 – Le Mans 1989
(5) Engine bay – 'Works' Mini Cooper S
(6) Ferrari Dino 246 – Goodwood
Revival 2006

(7) Talbot Lotus (Chrysler
UK)
(8) The sky is very
important to any artist.
Always keep a large
reference file on this subject
(9) Garage and street
furniture are important for
period subjects

④ Wheels, tyres & suspensions

Fig 4.1
Leader of the Pack
Acrylic on canvas
61 x 76.2cm/24 x 30in
Courtesy of Gilbert Adams

The snow-covered roads of the Alps Maritime are the backdrop to this composition, which depicts a Jaguar MKVII saloon being driven at high speed during the 1953 Monte Carlo Rally.
I was supplied with a photo reproduction. From this, I created a full-scale pencil rough, at the same time researching the variety of badges displayed across the Jaguar's front.
I have been lucky enough to have driven these very same roads and in the same conditions in recent years, so my photo archive was sourced for references. These big Jaguar saloons were powered by a 3.4 litre engine to push them along at over 100mph, but very little was done to the suspension for rallying, hence there was lots of body roll, with the offside wheel practically dangling in fresh air.
For the actual painting I used a fine, 100 per cent cotton canvas on stretchers. Although these commercially bought canvasses come already Gesso primed, I like to add at least two more coats of the same primer before I draw in my final composition.
Using vibrant blues against rich colours like Raw and Burnt Sienna helps give the painting sparkle, finally finishing with liberally applied slashes of Titanium White.

A ah, wheels! Yes, those are the round things with strips of black wrapped round them, stuck at the bottom of the car. A somewhat flippant description of a most important component of a vehicle that sometimes artists seem to treat with a degree of indifference.

The major problem is choosing the correct ellipse for the angle of the car. There is one simple rule: the axis of the ellipse is always at right angles to the car's axle centre line.

It is immaterial how the ellipse is created

Figs 4.2 (left) and 4.2/1 (below)
Wire wheels are without doubt the most difficult type of wheel to draw or paint. The human eye gets confused sorting out the jumble of lines which are the spokes. There are two rows of spokes radiating from the inner and outer hub, crossing over front to back and vice versa. These are arranged in such a way that, on the inner row, one set takes the car's acceleration stress, and the other takes the braking stress. The outer row bears the car's weight.
The most effective way to depict this type of wheel is to pick out the spokes in the light in white – i.e. the top of the front row – then, using blue or grey, depict those in the shadow.
For a wire wheel at speed, just the merest suggestion of the spokes is necessary, as shown in this rough sketch (fig 4.2/1).

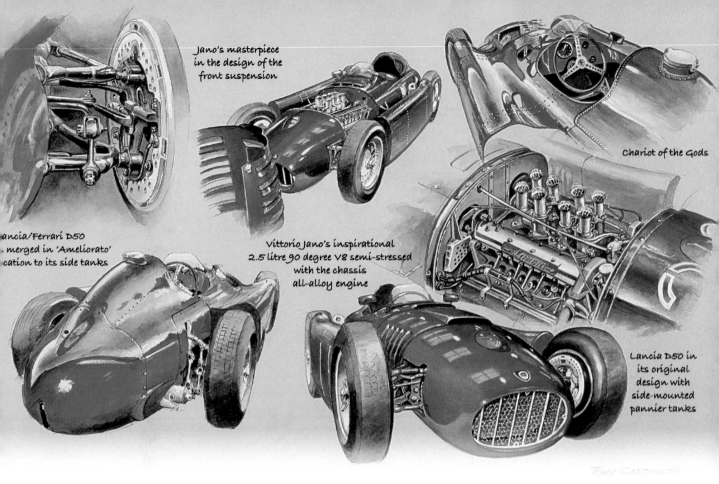

Jano's masterpiece
in the design of the
front suspension

Chariot of the Gods

Lancia/Ferrari D50
merged in 'Ameliorato'
cation to its side tanks

Vittorio Jano's inspirational
2.5 litre 90 degree V8 semi-stressed
with the chassis
all-alloy engine

Lancia D50 in
its original
design with
side-mounted
pannier tanks

Fig 4.3

The Lancia D50 and Lancia/Ferrari D50 Grand Prix
car of the mid-1950s are my all-time favourite racing
cars, although they were not all that successful in their
day, the all-conquering Mercedes-Benz W196, driven by
Fangio and Moss, was their main adversary.

This car, designed by Vittorio Jano, was an Italian
masterpiece in automobile engineering, the equivalent
of a Michelangelo sculpture. Everything on the car was
beautifully designed and made. Likewise, with this
replica built by a famous car restoration company.

I created these watercolour sketches from photographs
and sketches whilst on a visit to the builder's workshops.

First, I lightly drew in, using a 'B' pencil, the car's
basic outline and some detail, then gradually applied
the watercolour to create the appearance of the highly-
reflective paint finish of the car's bodywork. I find this
effect can be achieved by using Ultramarine Blue on
the upper surface blended into the actual colour with
Vermillion Red.

– most artists or illustrators can construct a basic
ellipse freehand – but for accuracy, I always use an
ellipse guide, a template created with every degree
of ellipse from 10 to 90 degrees, and sizes ranging
from 5mm to 200mm. Of course, this gives only
the correct basic angle, and you now have to set
about creating both the wheel and the tyre.

I find that once the ellipse of the outer wheel
rim has been drawn, and the inner rim where the
wheels' centre meets the rim has been decided,
the rest of the wheel can fall into place. It does
help to know the section through a wheel, and a
visit to your local tyre fitting depot can give you
some idea of how a wheel is constructed and how
the tyre fits within the rim section.

Now the tyres! There are basically two types
of tyre construction; cross-ply and radial-ply
(the former is used very little now, only for older
vehicles). These terms refer to how the tyre is
constructed with actual physical appearance of
the two being very similar, although the radial-ply
bulges more above the contact tread area. The
advantage of the radial-ply tyre is in cornering,
due to the flexible side wall and because all of the
tyre tread is constantly in contact with the road
surface.

Tyres have two major areas that the artist has
to portray – tread and side wall. Only the radial-ply

Fig 4.4
Current tyre design combines appearance with performance, especially when intended for cars such as the Subaru Impreza WRC.
If you decide to show a wheel and tyre in this position, i.e. the wheel turned towards you, remember that, in the highlighted portion, the tread pattern will be clearly visible if the car is shown static. If showing your subject at high speed, just a hint of the tread pattern is necessary.

Fig 4.5
Never before in everyday motoring have so many different alloy wheels been available. If you wish to embellish your artwork by changing the wheels from the original reference material, always make a careful note of the spoke spacings or the repeat patterns on the wheel.
Wheels play an important part in a car's appearance, so ensure these are correct as this will make all the difference to your finished piece.

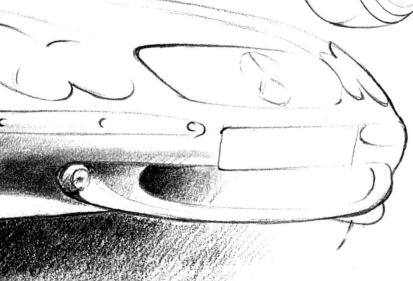

Fig 4.6
Here, in this pencil sketch is another example of a low profile, high-performance tyre fitted to an alloy wheel. Of course, like fig 4.4, you would only see tread detail if the wheel is shown turning.

First, make sure you have selected the correct wheel centre line and appropriate degree of ellipse. Next, construct the ellipse for the tread shoulder and the inner and outer wall ellipses which give the tyre's profile; lastly, construct the wheel rims and hubs.

Wheel centre line

Fig 4.7
The more traditional steel rim fitted with a chrome hub cap. Most standard production cars are still fitted with steel rims, although many now have plastic wheel trims, usually made to look like the more expensive alloy wheels. The same principle applies to constructing a drawing of this type of wheel and tyre as with the alloy, minus the spokes.

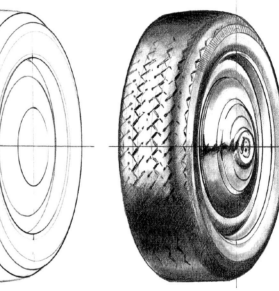

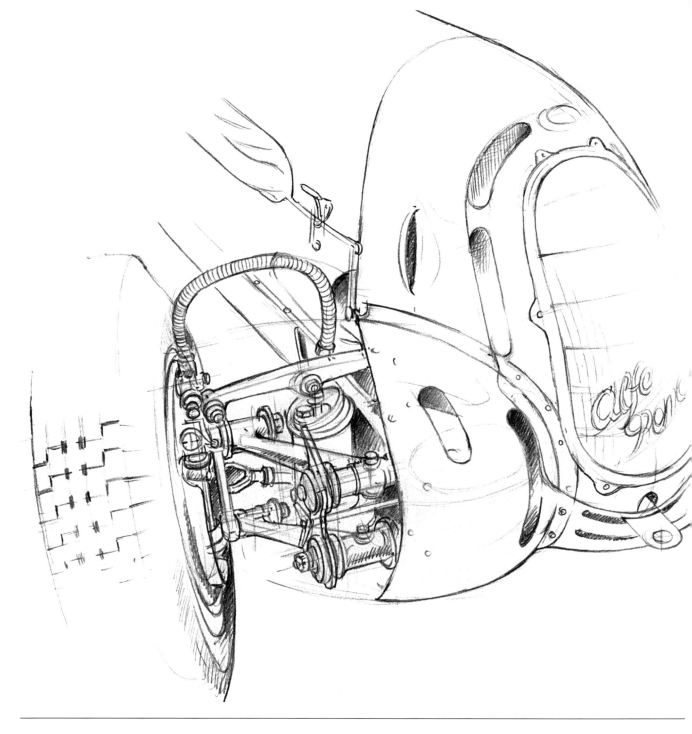

tyre tread pattern continues down part of the tyre wall, giving no hard shoulder as with the cross-ply. The current trend with tyres which has been with us for some years, is low-profile tyres, so low in some cases that the car appears to be running on a black rubber band when, even in the not-too-distant past, tyres had quite deep tyre walls. My advice to the student is to be observant, make notes, take photographs of wheels and tyres, and keep a selection on file for future reference.

    Now to another important component, the suspension, where technology has moved on in

Fig 4.8
I came across this Alfa Romeo 1937 Tipo C being worked on in the paddock at Goodwood, and couldn't resist making this pencil drawing of its front suspension – a double-wishbone fitted with a form of twin friction dampers.
Normally, you would never see this suspension exposed, as a section of bodywork hides it from view, but I thought it made an interesting sketch. It's all good practice to hone your draughtsmanship, plus give an understanding of the technical aspect of the workings of motorcars, especially those built for racing.

leaps and bounds. The reason for suspension is to absorb the lumps and bumps of uneven road surfaces. The system must have springiness for load and damping to absorb energy, hence the use of springs and dampers/shock absorbers.

From the very early beginnings of the motorcar, the leaf spring – directly descended from the horse-drawn carriage – was used on front and rear suspensions. Gradually, the front spring was replaced by double-wishbone or, later, McPherson strut assemblies. There are also other variations, one of which is the Hotchkiss drive which helps reduce prop shaft lift on bumps and consists of two leaf springs set as far apart as possible on the rear axle. Dampers/shock absorbers are then mounted at the same location as the leaf spring on the axle, with the top of the damper mounted to the car's bodywork.

The most common rear suspension assembly

Fig 4.9
By the mid-1960s, the double-wishbone on racing cars had been slimmed down, although still retaining the basic principles as in fig 4.8. The top wishbone of this 1964 Lotus 24 has now become virtually one piece with the lower section doing the fore and aft location work. This type of suspension layout was purely to save weight – all-important on a racing car.
When drawing cars of this type, be aware of the suspension links, as the top one is angled upward (known as dihedral).

Suspension. Top link

Dunlop racing tyres

heel re line

in use today is the trailing-arm, which
has two rear-facing wishbones with
a coil spring mounted between the
wishbone and the car's underbody, aided
by two dampers. Again, like the front suspension,
there are variations, such as the de Dion and
Mercedes-Benz systems; these are not commonly
used but the artist should be aware that such
systems may be fitted.

Where artists come face-to-face with
suspensions is when drawing and painting racing
cars, especially Formula One, as their suspension
systems are completely exposed; during the
1950s, Grand Prix cars carried polished double-
wishbones, whereas today's Grand Prix cars have
carbon fibre examples with an aerodynamic profile
on the upper wishbone.

Fig 4.10

Now, at the beginning of the 21st century, Formula One cars have embraced the use of carbon fibre in suspensions and bodywork, but the actual layout is still a modern version of the double-wishbone, with the arms of carbon fibre but designed as an aerofoil section to help the car's overall performance.

Today's designers have come to a completely opposite conclusion to that of those in the 1960s; slanting the top wishbones downward – known as adhedral – to give better driver 'feel'.

When painting examples of current Formula One cars, the suspension is black, so the upper surface takes on a blue tone. Likewise, tyres are virtually a cylinder, whether static or in motion. The lighter tones will be at the top, running down to the darkest tones at ground contact, using a Cobalt or Ultramarine Blue, going down to Paynes Grey and black. I also like to use Burnt Sienna in the mid range area – it helps to create a soft, rubber look.

Fig 4.11

When creating the basic drawing of wheels and tyres, as with fig 4.7, make sure you have the correct wheel centre line. Also, depending on your viewpoint, the ellipse angles change across the car as shown, starting with 10 degrees, through to a 25 degree ellipse on the outer tyre edge.

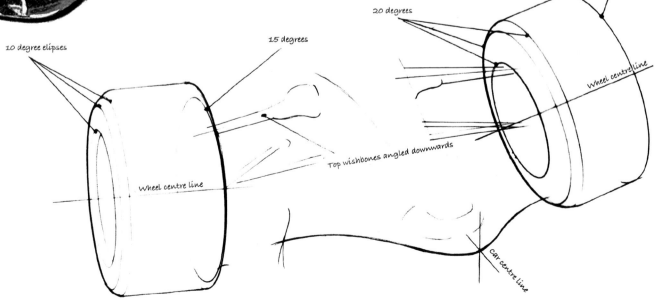

25 degrees

20 degrees

15 degrees

10 degree elipses

Wheel centre line

Wheel centre line

Top wishbones angled downwards

Car centre line

Fig 4.12
Marathon Triumph
Watercolour – Courtesy of Philip Young

I have included this watercolour vignette of a Triumph TR3A taken from a montage (original 20 x 30in) of rally cars, as an example of when 'Gremlin' gets to work; not once, but twice, in this case.

First, the usual problem is time, having a deadline to meet meant I was rushing. The overall illustration worked well with the Triumph as the main focus within the montage itself.

But the real mistake, which for me muted my satisfaction with the finished painting, was the 'wonky' nearside front wheel. Due to the time factor, I eyeballed this drawing of the wheel instead of using a 35 degree ellipse guide to create the correct angle, resulting in the wonky effect.

Do not let this occur as wheels can make or break your masterpiece, so get your ellipses sorted out before committing to the finished artwork.

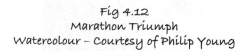

Gremlin will always try to give you 'wonky' wheels; choose the correct angle of ellipse.

esert duellers:-
ohn Dresser and Ian Bond TR3a

⑤ Reflections, light & shade

For obvious reasons, light and shade play an important part in any drawing or painting, and never more so than when depicting objects such as motorcars. The very nature of the motorcar, with its highly-polished reflective surfaces, can give endless opportunities to make good use of light and shade.

Once decided on the type of vehicle you are going to draw or paint – be it a sleek sports car or chunky four-wheel drive – you then have to decide on the direction of your light source. As an example, if drawing a car from a three-quarter front view, you do not want your light source coming from the top right as this will cast the

Fig 5.1
Red on Red
Watercolour, Bockingford 425gm
51 x 38cm/20 x 15in

Monaco is synonymous with money, glamour and fast cars, and I have been lucky enough to visit on numerous occasions, but never for the famous Grand Prix racing round its streets.

This watercolour painting depicts the two 'works' Lancia D50s of Ascari and Castellotti, blasting past the Hotel Mirabeau during the 1955 race, followed by the Ferrari of Farina.

To give contrast between light and shade, I used Phthalo Blue in the shadows, with Yellow Ochre and Burnt Sienna for the buildings in sunlight. For the Lancias in their Italian racing red, I used Vermillion (hue). To create the highly-polished surface of their bonnets, Ultramarine Blue was used to reflect the blue Mediterranean sky.

Fig 5.2
Automotive rendering project
Letraset Marker Paper
43 x 58cm/17 x 23in

Here are two typical examples of an automotive
rendering drawing. First, create a base
drawing on a Letraset bleedproof
marker pad using a fine line
black biro pen. Then, using
this as an underlay,
redraw it more
precisely as
an outline
drawing,
again on
Letraset or any
other bleedproof
paper.
When this phase
is complete, choose
a colour from the
'Magic Marker' range to suit your
particular creation and apply the marker
(in this case, black to areas like lower body sides,
glass reflection, wheels, tyres and under-car shadow).
Other markers have been used; i.e. cool grey on fig 2/1
and on fig 5.2/2, cool grey and warm greys plus reds
for tail lights, etc.
For the upper surfaces that reflect sky tones and
highlights, I used 'Conte' soft pastel sticks mixed with
talcum powder to allow the pastel to flow smoothly. First,
scrape the stick into a small pile of pastel and mix in
the talcum powder. Dip a cotton wool pad in the mix, rub
off the excess and apply to the car's upper surfaces with
clean sweeping strokes. Rub off the highlights with a
soft clean eraser. Set the pastel area
with spray fixative and then
repeat the process until
the required depth
of colour is
achieved.
Finally, flick
in dabs of
watercolour
Permanent
White with
a small
brush (01
or 02).

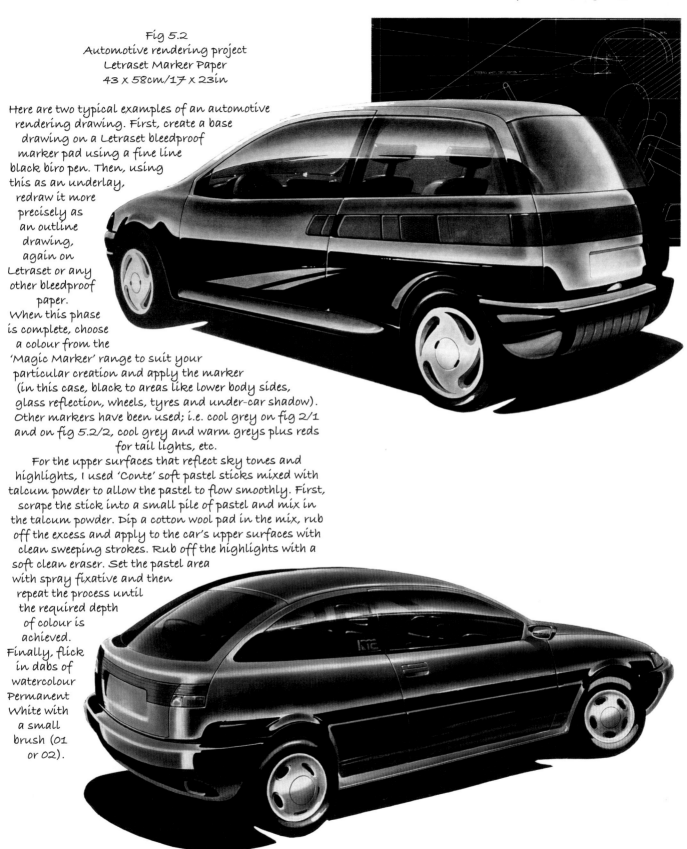

most important aspect of the car into shadow. The ideal direction is virtually directly overhead and slighty to the left.

Another aspect of the importance of light and shade is the colour of the automobile against the colour of the background. The best course of action is to select a contrasting colour, or one that is completely neutral.

One method of observing light and shade, apart from real life on a sunny day, is to create the conditions in miniature using a ⅛ scale model and a desk lamp fitted with a daylight bulb. Place the model on a curved sheet of thin white card so there are no edges showing (see fig 5.5), then, by changing the angle of the lamp to simulate the light source, you can observe the changing shadows and the light on the model's surface (see figs 5.5/1-5.5/3).

Beside the actual light, which could be artificial

Fig 5.3
Photo references were used to create this drawing of
a 1955 Buick Riviera on Royal Blue Daler-Rowney
Canford paper. The working drawing was created with
Stabilo Carbothello pastel pencils and soft graphite
pencils, 2B and a 5B, ensuring that proportions were
correct and that the overall appearance captured the
essence of one of America's all-time classic models.
The first step is to transfer the drawing onto the coloured
paper by rubbing white pastel on the back of a photocopy
of the original drawing. When this stage is complete,
enhance the transferred outline using a white pencil to
give a clear precise line. Then proceed to laying in the
tonal range and reflections and shade.
This model has a blue and white duo-tone colour scheme
typical of the mid-1950s, hence the use of blue paper as
the base colour. The first stage was to work in the white
areas of bodywork and some of the basic highlights: top
of the wings/fenders, bonnet/hood and roof. Blue areas
were enhanced with various shades of blue and black
pastel pencils to create reflections, etc. Apply the pastel
in stages, building up the depth of colour. Use spray
fixative before applying further pastel until you have
achieved the desired depth of colour. For this drawing, a
ground base of cobbled blocks, set in circular patterns
radiating from the front wheel, created a focal point.
Finally, to enhance the chrome work, white wall tyres
and pin points of highlights, use watercolour Titanium
White. By using coloured paper with a limited range of
pastel pencils you can create a very pleasing drawing.

60 degree elipse

61

Volvo XC 60

Fig 5.4
Volvo XC 60
Markers, pastels and
Biro pens

This sequence
demonstrates how to create an effective rendering similar
to fig 5.2, using only a ballpoint pen, marker pens of
studio quality (not permanent or dry markers), and
pastels, working on bleedproof marker paper.
First, create a rough pencil sketch of the car you wish to
portray. Once satisfied with the drawing, use this as an
underlay from which to create a more accurate outline
drawing using a fine line ballpoint pen on marker paper.
Before I explain the next phase, a word about marker pens.
The two I use are Magic Marker Twin Tip and Copic Ciao,
also twin tip. Neither is cheap to buy so always make
sure the caps are firmly in place when not in use so that
they do not dry out.
Both manufacturers have a range of about 150 colours
but for car illustrations I think only 20 are needed – the
definite colours being Cool Grey 1-9 and Warm Grey
1-9, Black, Deep Blue, Carmine Red and Orange; the last
two for indicators and tail lights.
The next phase is as described in paragraphs two and
three of Fig 5.2.

Figs 5.5-5.5/3
These four photos of a 1/8 scale model of a BMW Mini Cooper demonstrate how different lighting affects a car's appearance.

Fig 5.5 (below)
This virtually side-on view with the light source coming from the rear right side creates highlights on the upper section of the door and body panels, leaving the front area darker.

Fig 5.5/1 (bottom)
The direction of light coming from the front left casts reflective light on the bonnet surface, but leaves the side of the car in darkness.

if painting a night scene, another contributing factor to the light and colour of the automobile you are depicting is the location of your subject. Using a straightforward example: bright, sunny day, blue sky, green field with trees and a dark-coloured car (remember, the darker the colour of the car, the deeper the reflection). The top surfaces, bonnet/hood, roof, boot/trunk and upper areas of the wing and body sides will basically reflect sky tones (blue), whilst the lower body sides take on the colour of the immediate ground surface (green). The centre area of the side panels, plus the curves on upper surfaces, retain the colour of the car, whilst at waist level you would see the skyline with trees, buildings, etc. I have known

Light source

Light source

Light source

Light source

Fig 5.5/2 (top)
The light in this view is coming directly from the rear. Although it casts reflective light on the lower body side panels, it leaves the front end in relative shadow, which is not good for showing detail.

Fig 5.5/3 (above right)
In this view, the direction of the light source is the same as in 5.5/1, but is a more even light, showing up the car's front end whilst creating lighter tones on the car's side panels. This diffused light helps show the detail of the grille and headlamps and is more acceptable for creating a drawing or painting.

artists portray tongue-in-cheek scenes showing a camel train and the pyramids as a reflection in a car's side panels just to see if anybody would notice!

   At the other end of the colour range, white- or cream-painted cars give very subtle reflections, whilst yellow gives off nothing at all and really is the worst colour for the artist to illustrate.

Gremlin will have you on the verge of despair at times, but research, preparation and planning will send him packing.

Fig 5.6
Freelander 2
Cartridge paper 90gm – Pencil

All of today's 4x4s owe their very existence to the universal Jeep of World War Two, followed by the Land Rover and the German-built Unimog, both of which were developed in the late 1940s.
Therefore, I feel it appropriate to include some of these vehicles in this book but, must confess, other than the Jeep, I have very rarely been asked to portray this type of vehicle.
I found it interesting to create this pencil drawing of a Land Rover Freelander 2 because of its sheer brutal front end styling – its many surface changes create the opportunity to show and practice your skills with a pencil.
Again, with other examples in this book, the front end of the car is emphasised whilst letting the rear fade away. This puts all of the focus on the important area of your sketch.

Fig 5.7
Edwardian Racer 1906 Panhard-Levassor
Ink and wash drawing

This is an example of a simple drawing using a basic
pen dipped in waterproof ink, and watercolours Peat
Brown and Van Dyke Brown.
Create a very light pencil sketch, then develop the
ink line drawing quickly by eye and apply the
wash tones in a loose style – a mix of ink and
watercolour. This style of drawing can be used to
create very interesting vignettes within the pages
of books and magazines.

Fig 5.8
1966 Morris Mini Cooper 'S'
Watercolour

With any medium you can
create the appearance of a
highly-polished painted
surface. The trick is in
the contrast of tones
and using reflections to
accentuate the car's colour.
Whatever colour a vehicle
is, it always takes on
some of the colour from
its surroundings; i.e. the
lower body panels will take
on ground colours to about
halfway up the body side,
whilst all of the upper surfaces
reflect sky.

Fig 5.9
Mercedes-Benz, A New Dawn

When inspiration strikes, the initial reaction is to create a rough impression of the finished subject. This composition is depicting a Mercedes CR9 coming out of the Mulsanne corner, past the famous signalling pits, in the early morning light of the 1989 Le Mans 24 hour race. I was fortunate to be at this particular race, taking many photographs for future reference. Hence, the creation of this rough draft is the last in a series of six depicting the history of Mercedes-Benz in motorsport.

To create this image I used 70gm Daler-Rowney bleedproof marker paper, with a Magic Marker (twin tip) and markers ranging through the cool greys; C1-C5, warm grey, W2 and W4 in the background, with details and shadows in black marker and black crayon pencil.

All of the highlights were created using Permanent White gouache.

The ultimate trick is to try not to lose the spontaneity created in the rough draft. This illustration will eventually form a pair of paintings with fig 2.10; same size and medium.

Yellow Ochre

Light

Raw
Sienna

Shade

Vermillion Red

What I have described in the preceding paragraphs is only the basic colours you might expect to see and use but these have to be blended in subtle tones from dark to light shades, plus highlights where necessary (see fig 5.7).

The basis for creating a pleasing and satisfying image of a car's surface appearance is simply do not use streaks of colour, just basic shades with blended tones round the edges. If you create too many broken images of colours it acts like camouflage as used in wartime on vehicles, aircraft and ships, breaking up the outline and thus destroying the effect you are trying to create.

Within this chapter, I will show you examples of all the methods that can be used to achieve a very slick and professional-looking drawing or painting.

Shade
Light source

Shade

Windsor Blue (Red shade)
Burnt Sienna

Figs 5.10, 5.11 & 5.12
These next three sketches were inspirational and instantly put down on paper before the scene disappeared from my mind.

Fig 5.10 (opposite)
This is a Ferrari 250 GT Tour de France model, blasting through the streets of the ancient city of Bologna during the Mille Miglia, the famous Italian road race. I used warm colours to create the effect of sunlight on the buildings and cool blue in shaded areas.
To get the areas of contrast, I produced this quick wash sketch using a fine line pen and Paynes Grey watercolour. For any composition it is always best to first create a thumbnail sketch of your idea. This one is only 7½ x 6¾in/19cm x 17cm. From this, a more detailed drawing can be produced.

Fig 5.11
Again, I have produced a very quick, small pencil sketch for a future large-scale painting. The effect I want to achieve is a patch of sunlight illuminating the main subject, a Jaguar Mk 9 saloon, contrasting with dark rainclouds in the background.

De Soto Adventurer.

Fig 5.12
These are the initial working roughs for an intended painting in acrylic on canvas. After producing the initial working rough (see insert), I produced a much larger watercolour rough, firming up the composition and colour.

Both of these need more work on the car and locomotive before committing to the final painting. Also, in the final composition, a mounted figure, say, a cowboy, might be added to the left foreground to give more interest.

The subject is a 1958 De Soto Adventurer convertible meeting a huge articulated Challenger locomotive operated by Union Pacific, 'highballing' across Wyoming hauling a freight train.

⑥ Headlamps & radiator grilles

I must explain from the start of this chapter that there is no such thing as a car headlight, it is a headlamp.

Ref: source – *Oxford English Dictionary*
Lamp – an electric, oil or gas device for giving light.
Origin – Greek Lampus – 'torch'.
Light – the natural form of energy that makes things visible – provide with light, not heavy.
The lamp is the source. Light is the product emitted from the lamp.

The early headlamps were lit by acetylene or oil, and were essentially a variation of coaching lamps. Electric-powered lamps appeared in America by 1904, with a dipping system fitted around 1915 in Cadillacs.

Headlamps became more efficient as car electrics and associated components, such as bulbs and reflectors, improved. In 1940 the round 7 inch (178mm) sealed beam headlamp became a standard requirement in most countries around the world, and by the late 1950s, American car designers had produced models with quad 5¾ inch lamps. The outer lamps provided the main beam and the inner lamps the dipped beams, giving the four-lamp look. British cars that used this system were the Triumph Vitesse and 2000 models, Humber Super Snipe, and some Bentleys. European manufacturers chose the stacked system, the low beam being the higher lamp with the lower the main beam. Mercedes-Benz and Facel Vega took this styling route.

Fig 6.2
These pencil sketches show in detail what you can expect to see on veteran, vintage and classic cars.
Below is an oil side lamp, manufactured between 1907 and 1912 and made of brass. In reality, they were fitted to motorcars long after these dates. The drawing, right, shows an ccetylene gas headlamp, manufactured during roughly the same period of 1904-1914. These were stirrup-mounted for ease of removal for cleaning and charging with Carbide.

Acetylene gas headlamps
1904 - 1914

Fig 6.1 (opposite)
Race to the West
Acrylic on canvas board
57 x 76cm/20 x 30in

The inspiration behind this painting was slightly more exotic, insomuch as, although the subject involved a Bentley racing a train, its destination was the French Riviera.
England's own Riviera is, of course, the south west of the country, mainly Devon and Cornwall, which is why I chose 'The Cornish Riviera Limited', a famous train of the steam era. At some point along the route between London and Penzance, I needed road and rail to come together, and the only spot I could find was near Slough, where the A4 and the Great Western Railway run parallel for a short stretch.
I wanted the Bentley to be a typical road-going example of the late 1930s, but painted in racing green, whilst the locomotive used was the Great Western King class.
The painting needed to be dramatic, hence the acute perspective allowing the Bentley to be shown virtually head-on, giving the impression that, at this point, car and train were racing neck-and-neck.

Oil side lamp circa
1907

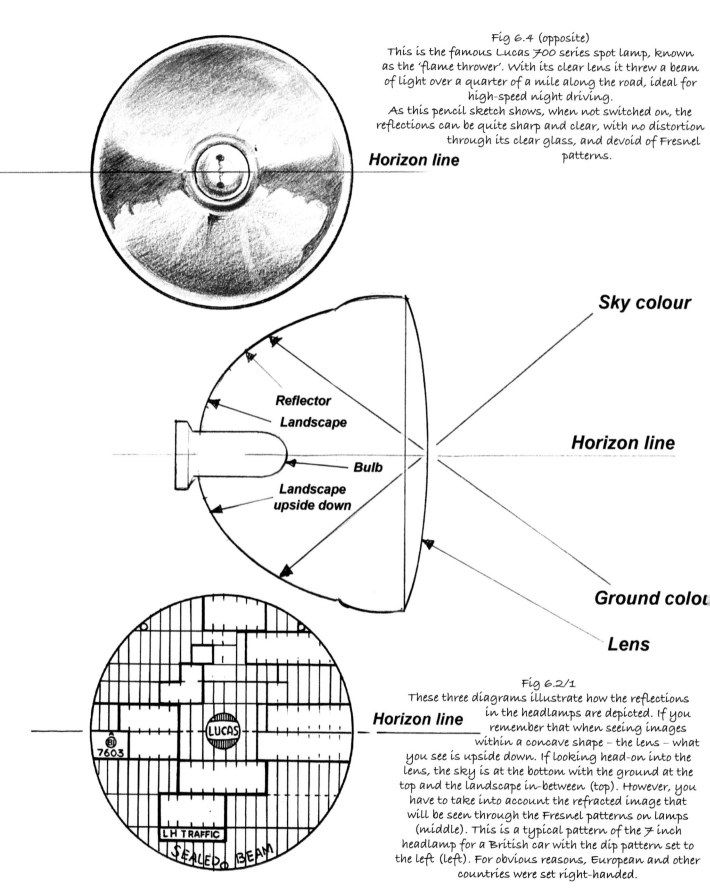

Horizon line

Fig 6.4 (opposite)
This is the famous Lucas 700 series spot lamp, known as the 'flame thrower'. With its clear lens it threw a beam of light over a quarter of a mile along the road, ideal for high-speed night driving.
As this pencil sketch shows, when not switched on, the reflections can be quite sharp and clear, with no distortion through its clear glass, and devoid of Fresnel patterns.

Sky colour

Reflector

Landscape

Horizon line

Bulb

Landscape upside down

Ground colour

Lens

Horizon line

Fig 6.2/1
These three diagrams illustrate how the reflections in the headlamps are depicted. If you remember that when seeing images within a concave shape – the lens – what you see is upside down. If looking head-on into the lens, the sky is at the bottom with the ground at the top and the landscape in-between (top). However, you have to take into account the refracted image that will be seen through the Fresnel patterns on lamps (middle). This is a typical pattern of the 7 inch headlamp for a British car with the dip pattern set to the left (left). For obvious reasons, European and other countries were set right-handed.

LUCAS
7603
LH TRAFFIC
SEALED BEAM

Fig 6.3
Austin-Healey 3000, RAC Rally 1965
Daler Line & Wash Board Gouache
51 x 76cm/20 x 30in
Courtesy of Marilyn Elliott

This painting of an Austin-Healey 3000 on the RAC Rally shows the typical layout of auxiliary lamps on a rally car of that period. The three lamps across the front are fog versions with a patterned lens, and the two mounted on the bonnet are 5 inch headlamps taken from another model. You can see in this painting how reflections create the concave shape of the auxiliary lamp reflectors.

Fig 6.6
This pencil sketch shows a typical car of the late 1960s, designed with a quad headlamp configuration built by Gordon Keeble. The headlamps are of the conventional reflector $5^3/4$ inch type, with separate sides and indicators placed below the main lights.
The style of this car's front end – its grille, headlamps, sidelights, bumpers, etc – became known as 'Chinese Eyes' by the car's designers.

Fig 6.5
This detail of the main painting on page 74 shows how the use of colour can replicate the nickel-plated surface of the reflectors of these massive, 10 inch Lucas headlamps; likewise with the spot lamps. By picking up on the surrounding colour you can achieve realistic-looking headlamps.
On early lamps, sheer size alone gave massive beams of light without the help of Fresnel patches. This type of headlamp was mostly fitted to powerful sports cars or sporting saloons of the period between 1920 and 1939, although some luxury limousines had them into the early 1950s.

The next big improvement came in 1962 with the introduction of the Halogen lamp, produced and developed by European companies such as Cibie, Bosche, and Lucas in the United Kingdom. These were much favoured by rally drivers as they virtually turned night into day. For artists, this meant portraying headlamps as pure white rather than a creamy mix.

With so many changes occurring throughout the history of the car, the artist must stay aware of what model had what and when, as detail accuracy is all-important and makes all the difference between producing a good or bad painting.

By the late 1960s and into the early 1970s, car manufacturers had begun to use rectangular headlamps, although the technology behind them was basically the same as round lamps, with a reflector dispersing the light through Fresnel patches on the lens in a precisely defined way (Fresnel patches are patterns on the glass lens).

Over the following decades until the present

Fig 6.7
Marathon MGB
Daler Superline Board

This illustration is unusual as the tone is laid on as a mechanical tint, cut out using a scalpel and laid in position on the line drawing.

The line drawing includes the outline of the car, grille, bumpers, lights, rally plate, competition number, wipers, windscreen, etc, plus hand-drawn dot tone on the outer spot lamp covers and tyres. All other tone is Letraset mechanical tone bought in sheet form.

You can use this to great effect to create the reflections in headlamps and spot lamps – use darker tones at the top – road surface and the lower half – leaving a white or lighter tone for the sky, plus hand-drawing black areas to sharpen reflections. Again, for what I call a technical pictorial drawing, I would recommend the use of all the usual drawing aids, such as french curves, sweeps, ellipse guides, etc.

Fig 6.7/1 (left)
These are just a few examples of the Manga Art range of Screen Tonesheets available to create artwork as shown in fig 6.7 and fig 7.3. All of these can be ordered from High Street graphics, craft or Manga Art shops. You can also purchase this product direct from the manufacturer, Letraset.

Screen Tone
MT214 10%
16.75/cm

Screen Tone
MT215 20%
16.75/cm

Screen Tone
MT217 40%
16.75/cm

Screen Tone
MT219 10%
25.5/cm

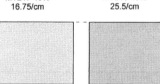

Screen Tone MT44
20% 23.5/cm

Screen Tone MT45
30% 23.5/cm

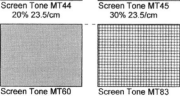

Screen Tone MT60
40% 33.5/cm

Screen Tone MT83

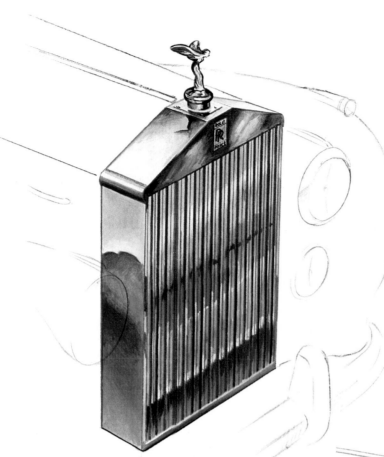

Fig 6.8
These two stylised paintings of classic-design radiators – a 1951 Rolls Royce Silver Wraith and a 1936 American-built Duesenberg – show over-exaggerated reflections. If you study examples of such radiators, however, you will see reflections very similar to those portrayed here.
In reality, they reflect the car they are attached to and some of its surroundings, such as the sky, landscape, and ground surface.
Visit museums and classic car rallies to see examples of various radiator and grille styles. Take photographs to build a good pictorial library for future reference, as you never know when you could be asked to paint some obscure model.

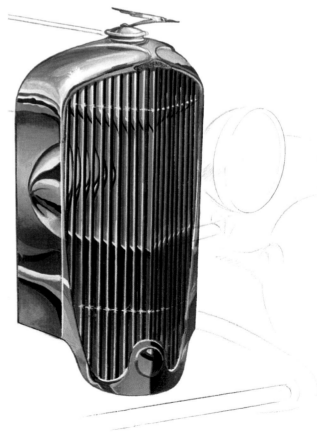

day, car headlamp designs became whackier, made possible by the use of injection moulding which enabled the current designs and shapes to be produced more cheaply.

Whereas once headlamps were only circular, now they come in all shapes and sizes, which makes it even more important for the artist to study them to ensure accuracy when drawing and painting current cars. Within the diverse shape of the overall headlamp unit, however, the actual lamp is still circular.

The other major feature of a car's frontal appearance is the grille. On early motorcars, this was dominated by the actual water-filled radiator, though there were exceptions – those that ran on steam, such as the Stanley or White – and those which were air-cooled, like the 1901 Lanchester.

Gradually, as cars became more sophisticated, designers hid the radiator behind lavish chrome

Fig 6.9
The designers of sports racing cars of the 1950s, trying to create smooth aerodynamic body shapes in the quest for high speed, made the headlamp disappear under clear covers that were an integral part of the body shape. This is illustrated here in this detail of a headlamp on the famous Jaguar D Type.
The lamps were of the conventional reflector type: chrome concave reflectors with Freznel patterned lenses. When drawing or painting cars of this period, the artist has to create double reflections; first the lamp unit and then the cover. Again, it's all down to observing what effect reflections and light have on the vehicle's body shape.

Gremlin will try to make you purchase unnecessary equipment: buy wisely ...

Fig 6.10 (right)
This quick watercolour sketch depicts a Porsche 956
Group C driven by Brun, Von Bayern and Atkin,
competing in the 1984 Le Mans 24 hour race.
As the car is white, the low evening sun casts blue
shadows across its front, with the side facing the sun
turning a warm off-white.
Cars like this have conventional round headlamps
under clear Perspex covers, so not only do you see the
usual reflections in the round headlamps, but also the
additional reflections in the shaped covers.
The reddy/brown colour on the car's front is the blood
from millions of dead insects. This, too, the artist has to
be aware of because, toward the end of most long distance
motor races, this – and road and brake dust – will
combine to give a dirty appearance.

Fig 6.11 (left)
The headlamps I have shown in this watercolour sketch of the latest BMW One series are known as Projector (polyellipsoidal) Lamps. These have been around since 1983 but it is only in recent years that nearly all production cars have been fitted with these units. There is no point going into the technicalities of these lamps because it has no bearing on drawing them. Rather like the Porsche 956 (fig 6.9), the shaded lamp covers are clear glass with reflections, and the Projector units are deep-set; unlit, they appear quite dark, unlike the reflector-type with Fresnel patterns on the actual lens.

Fig 6.12
Italian Glory
Watercolour
38 x 51cm/15 x 20in

I have always been in awe of Italy's mighty Mille Miglia road race. I created this painting of Gendebien and Wascher driving the famous Ferrari 250 GT Tour de France to victory in the GT category – they were also 3rd overall in the very last race held in 1957.

This subject shows that, when painting cars, you have to be skilled in other areas, too – in this case, architecture, which involves perspective and recession (see also fig 3.6).

For the Italian feel of the painting, I researched the towns and cities that the race passed through, and chose the old city gates of Bologna as the background.

Another aspect of this painting was how to depict headlamps ablaze in daylight. The simplest method is to leave the white, adding a hint of yellow and soft edges to the headlamp lens.

Fig 6.13
This line and wash drawing depicts a Sunbeam Rapier (top left), an Austin-Healey 3000 (bottom), and a Jaguar XK120 Roadster, all typical examples of 1950s and 1960s cars with standard 7 inch/178mm round headlamps, plus, 7 inch/178mm and 5 inch/128mm auxiliary lamps.
Half-tone line and wash drawing is a very effective technique for reproduction purposes.
First, choose your subjects and draw them as individual sketches, before mating them to create a montage.
Next, ink your pencil line work before adding the final watercolour wash using various wash tones of black only, or any other base colour you like.

grilles. Latterly, ducts and slots are used to feed air to that all-important component.

For the artist, getting the frontal appearance correct is crucial in order to create a successful painting. Other details, such as side lights, bumpers, overriders and even badges, will contribute greatly to the accurate, pleasing representation of the make and model car you are depicting.

Within this section, I will endeavour to explain the art of painting headlamps, with examples of early coaching-type lamps, right through to the current trend of Projector (polyellipsoidal) lamps, and how best to portray them. Likewise, grille design and a car's general frontal appearance.

Within the quest for more aerodynamic car body shapes, headlamps had to be accommodated behind clear covers, flared in to match the car's aerodynamic shape, as can be seen on models such as the Jaguar D Type, Ferrari Testa Rossa, and today's Group C sports cars.

7 Techniques & mediums

Style: - (1) A way of doing something. (2) A distinctive appearance, design or arrangement, and (3) A way of painting, writing, etc.
Technique: - (1) A particular way of doing something, especially something requiring special skills. (2) A person's level of practical skill.
Source: *Oxford English Dictionary*.

I think the above sums up this chapter, which is about creating a recognisable style unique to the artist, although I have found through experience that sometimes it pays to be versatile in this area. Although your style gets your work recognised, being able to create drawings, paintings, etc, in any medium and a variety of styles can secure you a lot more commissions in the long run.

I use whatever medium the subject or client demands. You still have to start somewhere, of course, and the obvious way is to use a pencil, with which it is easier to acquire the basic skills of drawing, as it is a medium that we have all grown

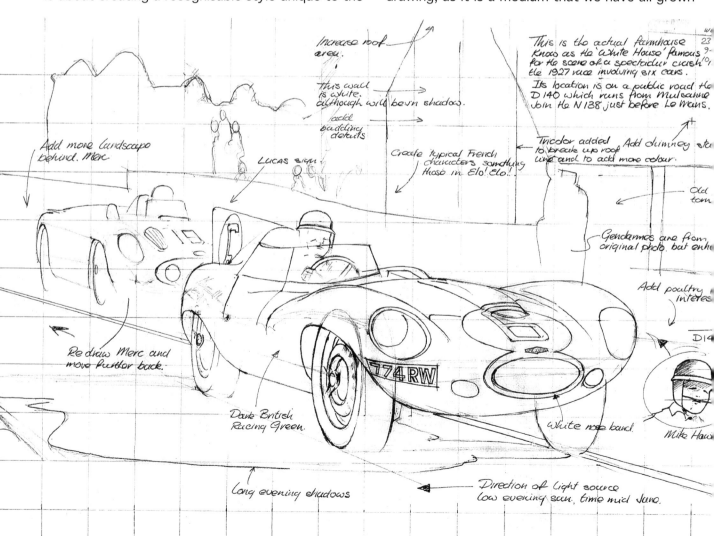

Increase roof area.

This wall is white. although will have barn shadows.

add budding details

Add more landscape behind. Merc.

LUCAS sign

Create typical French characters something those in Elo! Elo!

This is the actual farmhouse known as the 'White House' famous for the scene of a spectacular crash in the 1927 race involving six cars.

Its location is on a public road the D140 which runs from Mulsanne join the N138 just before Le Mans.

Tricolor added to break up roof line and to add more colour.

Add chimney sta

Old tom

Gendarmes are from original photo, but enha

Add poultry interes

D14

Re draw Merc and move further back.

Dark British Racing Green.

174 RW

White nose band

Mike Haw

Long evening shadows

Direction of light source low evening sun, time mid June.

up with and has been with us for centuries. Colour pencils can be used to great effect, too, but they must be soft enough to allow a graduation in tone, though also firm enough to create a sharp line.

Another versatile drawing aid is the fine line marker pen, which produces lines ideal for quick sketching. As you become more comfortable with using these pens, and if you are quick before the ink dries, you can wash over the work with a little water to achieve quite pleasing effects. Drawing with pen and ink, as with the pencil, has been with us for centuries but recent developments with inks have transformed this medium. Apart from the conventional 'Indian ink', which is waterproof, there are now water-soluble inks in many colours with which exciting drawings in line and wash can be created. As for the pens, I recommend the traditional nib range and the use of Chinese brushes to create a line and wash drawing. I do not subscribe to the notion that to achieve acceptable and professional standards within art you have to use the most expensive materials; just use the best your budget will allow! Remember, once, our ancestors drew on cave walls with sticks dipped

in ox blood and plant dyes, so, in theory, it should be possible to create a drawing or painting from whatever tools and material are available.

The marker pen is another medium which can be used to great effect. Most artists have their favourite brand; the two I use – 'Magic Markers' and 'Pantone' – are within a comprehensive range that includes a 'cool grey' and 'warm grey', plus other colours. These brands are probably the two most used by professionals, but there are others to choose from.

Yet another medium is pastels, which can produce effective and dynamic results when combined with markers, as well as being used in their own right. I have used this medium very rarely, though pastels, in conjunction with coloured Canson paper, can give some pleasing effects.

In terms of materials, I suppose most of us start with a box of watercolours, which, in reality, is the most difficult and demanding of all the mediums as there is no room for error. On the plus side, I have used this medium for many years because you can turn out clean drawings and paintings quite quickly.

continued page 98

Fig 7.1/2
76 x 51cm/30 x 20in

Full-size working pencil drawing of the final painting (fig 7.1). See main caption overleaf.

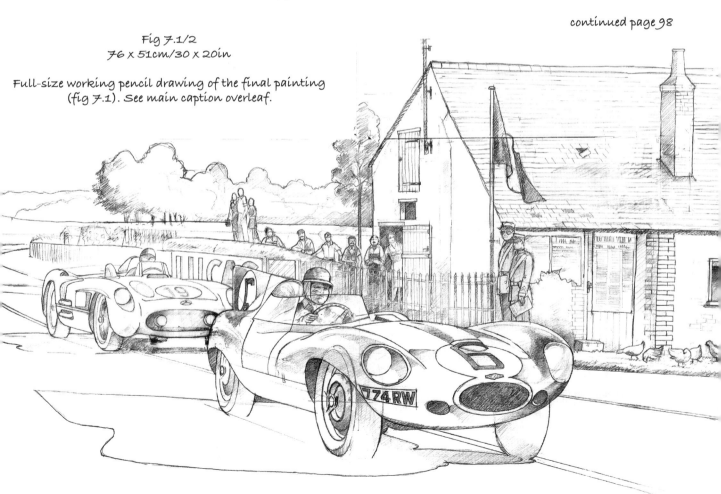

Fig 7.1
Jaguar Victory, Le Mans 1955
Watercolour, Bockingford 300gm tinted paper
78 x 51cm/30 x 20in

One of my all-time favourite sports racing cars, the famous D Type Jaguar. I have depicted the factory-entered car, resplendent in British Racing Green, driven by Mike Hawthorn and Ivor Bueb (the eventual winners), and chased by the Mercedes-Benz 300 SLR of Juan Manuel Fangio and Stirling Moss during the 1955 Le Mans 24 hour endurance race.

First, I created a sketch of the basic composition in A3 size (fig 7.1/1), and then enlarged it to the actual finished size, adding detail such as the figures, chickens, and building in the background known as the 'White House' (fig 7.1/2).

With all of the historical detail in place, the drawing was transferred onto a biscuit tint 300gm watercolour paper. This was chosen to give the painting a warm overall hue to help represent the colours associated with the sunset of a June evening.

I wanted to create more subtle tones rather than bright gaudy colours to represent the sunset. For the overall evening sky colour I chose Cadmium Yellow with a hint of Rose Madder (hue). Whilst the paper was still wet, I applied a little Paynes Grey and Ultramarine Blue. For the distant background I chose more Paynes Grey, with the near building and surroundings a mix of burnt Sienna, Yellow Ochre, Paynes Grey and Phthalo Blue. The road was as per the sky tones, with the Jaguar a mix of Phthalo Green and Winsor Green (blue/green), highlighted with the Cadmium Yellow Rose Madder mix, plus Ultramarine Blue.

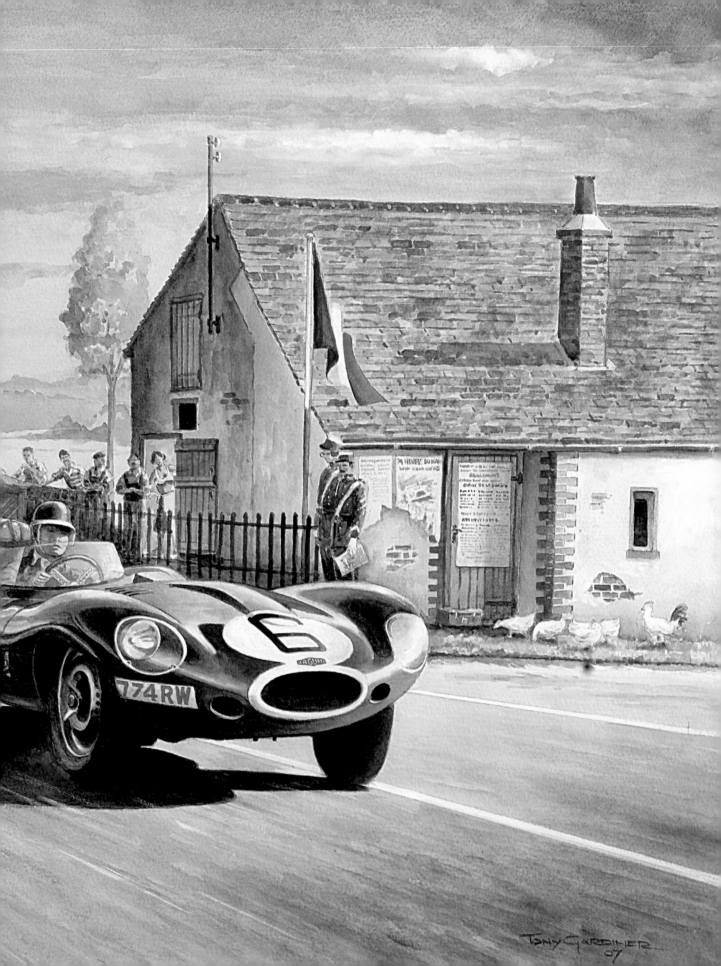

Fig 7.2 (below)
The Daily Telegraph
Weekend motoring supplement
1997 Peking to Paris

I have included this rough layout as an example of how editors
want to see an idea before committing to print. It is laid out the
same size as the paper's actual page size; i.e. broadsheet 36cm x
59cm, although it was only the width that concerned me. For the
actual rough sketch, I worked on a Letraset marker pad using
cool and warm greys from the Magic Marker range, and drawing
all the line work in black ballpoint pen.

The line and watercolour wash illustration had already been
completed for the client, *The Daily Telegraph*. Commission was
an added bonus as we could scan the original artwork with very
little modification necessary. The actual size of the original
artwork was 18 x 27in/45.6 x 68.4cm on Bockingford 300gm
paper. After selecting from old photos, the ones that would best
fit the composition were drawn down, then inked in with Sepia
waterproof ink using a traditional pen/nib, leaving space to fit
the repros of articles from *The Daily Telegraph* of 1907.

To create the feel of an old drawing, I laid a wash of Burnt
Sienna, then gradually added deeper tones of Burnt Sienna
and Sepia, plus very pale colours to the cars
and over the entire illustration.

Fig 7.2/1
Courtesy of *The Daily Telegraph*
& Philip Young

This is the actual illustration as
published in the weekend *Telegraph* of
14th January 1995. In this case, the
final layout and colour illustration
was exactly as per my original concept
sketch.

Fig 7.3
Porsche 911 and 914

These examples of two Porsche variants were created in the same way as fig 6.7 in the previous chapter, but not using as much tonal variation. They had to be kept clean and simple for a sharp reproduction image on the front cover of a workshop manual, hence, crisp line work, and tone kept to a minimum, with black areas to give it 'punch'.

Fig 7.4 (opposite bottom)
Return to Monte Carlo
Courtesy of Jeremy Dickson
(Classic Rally Association)

This was produced as a limited edition
print.
Creating a watercolour montage such
as this is no different to creating any
other watercolour painting, although each
individual vignette should work together
as a whole.
I like to start top left so the composition
flows across the picture area, finishing
bottom right (see fig 7.4/1, right). Draw
each car individually and move them
around until they're arranged in the
desired layout. I like to include as much
landscape as possible because it helps
to give more atmosphere to the overall
composition.
When applying the medium you are using, make sure
each vignette blends together, though at the same time is
able to stand alone if required (see fig 7.4/2, below).

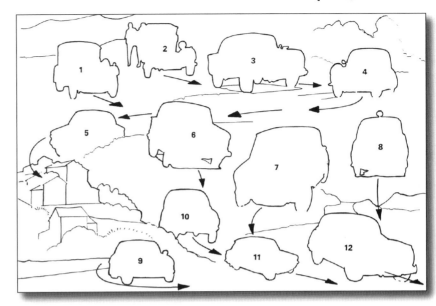

Fig 7.5
Vauxhall VX220 (colour scheme)
Courtesy of Andrew Duerden – Vauxhall Motorsport
Letraset marker paper
23 x 35cm/9 x 14in

Sometimes, clients need a quick response to a request for a piece of artwork. The only option the artist has when this happens is to create an image using the quickest method at his disposal. In this case, I decided on a marker pen rendering.

The client, Vauxhall Motorsport, was seeking an idea for a colour scheme for the Vauxhall VX220, which was to enter the British Hillclimb Championship driven by Tiff Needell, which reflected the colour scheme already in use on its Vectra saloons that were racing at the time.
For me, the quickest route was to use one of Vauxhall's publicity photographs to create a rough line drawing (fig 7.6/1), adding the colour scheme in marker and crayon. These sort of sketches literally take minutes to produce because they are no more than throwaway colour notes.

Fig 7.5/2
Vauxhall VX220
Bockingford 300gm watercolour paper
43 x 53cm/17 x 21in

The colour sketch of the proposed colour scheme was chosen with some slight modification. I then proceeded to make a more accurate pencil drawing of the VX220 on a slightly larger scale, transferring this onto watercolour paper, drawing in the outline only.
I then masked off the car's shape with Windsor and Newton Art Masking Fluid so that I could apply an overall Vermillion wash as the background colour. After letting the background dry thoroughly, I gently removed the masking fluid – which is, in fact, Latex – by lightly rubbing with my fingers, leaving white paper. I drew in the car's details and painted the required colours. Lastly, I turned my attention to creating the reflection.
The photo shows the finished artwork still stretched on the backing board.

Gremlin will always try to make you overwork your masterpiece: resist this temptation.

Fig 7.6
1965 Mini Cooper 'S'
Frisk CS10 Line Surface Board (Media 6)

Ink drawings were used extensively in the advertising media during the 1950s and 1960s, mainly because of the poor quality of newsprint paper. Illustrators learnt how to draw clean, crisp ink drawings for better reproduction qualities.

What the illustrator has to decide is how certain tones in the black and white or colour photograph are interpreted with ink line. Obviously, the darker the tone the more intense the ink line, be it in the form of cross hatching, dots, lines (thick and thin), or solid.

For this type of work I prefer to use Rotring drawing pens, 0.25 and 0.35, with Rotring drawing ink which prevents these pens from clogging. Due to the nature of a drawing of this type, I recommend the use of drawing aids to create crisp lines; i.e. ellipse guides and french curves.

Fig 7.7 (opposite)
The Great Trials Lands End, Exeter and Edinburgh
Daler Line and Wash Board
Courtesy of Philip Young

This is a piece of artwork that was commissioned for a motoring journal. The first priority was to conduct some research into these three famous motor events.

The artist and the client have to agree on a cross-section of typical cars seen on these events.

The next process is to draw the subjects lightly, using an F or H pencil. When the entire layout is finished, apply a weak wash of Sepia watercolour over the whole area to provide a light background colour. Next, ink in the pencil drawing using Sepia and Nut Brown Windsor & Newton Drawing Ink (all of the tones were created with a mix of these two inks), with a soft, flexible drawing nib in a traditional holder.

For certain areas I wanted to create a muddy effect. This was achieved with a splatter texture by dipping an old toothbrush into the ink and lightly flicking the bristles – do not apply too much as you can end up with a big blob!

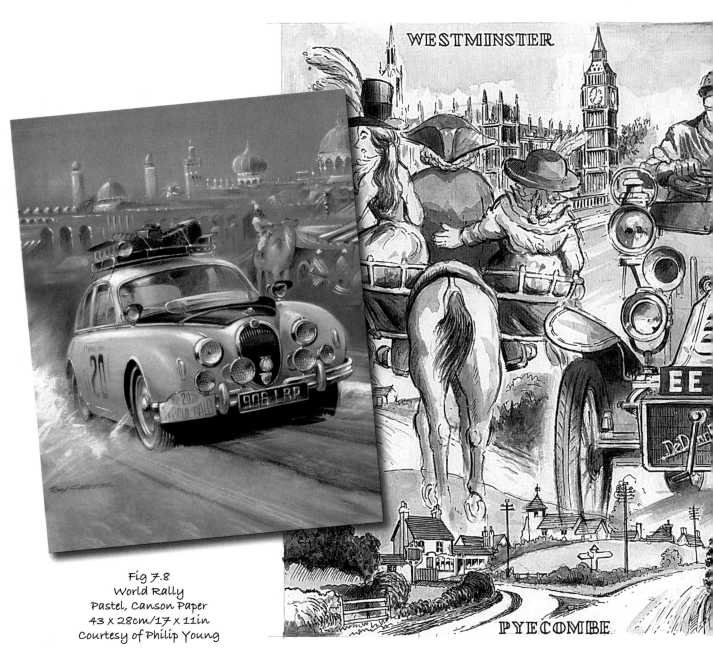

Fig 7.8
World Rally
Pastel, Canson Paper
43 x 28cm/17 x 11in
Courtesy of Philip Young

I have very rarely used pastels for
a drawing of this nature, but in this case, the subject
suited this medium as the client required a hot, dusty,
dry appearance.
I selected Mid Tan pastel paper from the Canson range,
and, for complete contrast, white for the car. I drew the
composition in white pastel crayon, using Permanent
White watercolour for the car's highlights, and black
marker for shadow and detail on the bonnet, grille and
roof luggage.
The odd detail in the background was drawn lightly
with black crayon, then highlights were added with white
pastel and watercolour. Finally, to give the impression of
the car driving at high speed, I dry-brushed in flicks of
Permanent White Designer's gouache.

Watercolour choice is quite comprehensive,
with pans and tubes and a variety of colour ranges
and prices to suit all pockets – there are at least
ten brands on the market, giving the artist a wide
selection.

The last medium covered in this chapter is
acrylics, which give amazing results very similar to
oil paints. The same techniques can be applied to
both, but remember that oils take longer to dry.

Whichever way you approach painting with
acrylics – loose-style or a highly detailed piece of
work – you will find them most rewarding. I like
to use Daler-Rowney 'Cryla' colour or 'System 3'
acrylics, plus System 3 brushes. Manufacturers

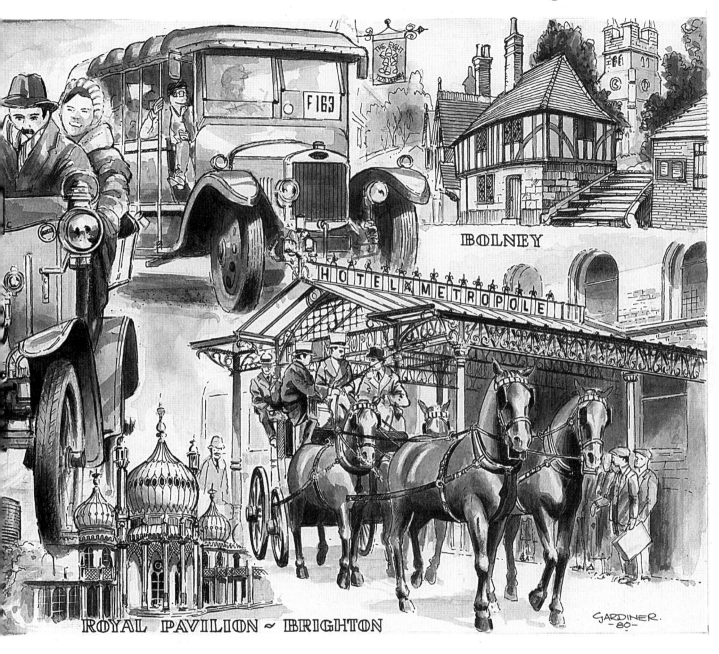

Fig 7.9
The Brighton Road
Line & Wash Half-Tone
19 x 44cm/7¹/₂ x 13¹/₂in
Courtesy of *The Motor*

Your skills as an artist should take you beyond
painting cars only, because, as previously stated, cars do
not exist in isolation.
I was commissioned by a well-known motoring
magazine to create this drawing to accompany an article
on the famous London to Brighton Veteran Car Run,
which takes place annually every November.

For the first piece of research, I checked the route to
see what interesting landmarks it passes through.
Secondly, I found out what other events took place on the
same stretch of road. Thirdly, I mated them all together
to form an interesting composition in the space allowed,
gradually linking together each vignette in a suitable
arrangement.
The process then is to lightly pencil in with an HB or
F pencil, and ink in the drawings using a Rotring
0.25 pen. Jet Black was used for the half-tone wash
watercolour. Begin with pale washes, gradually applying
more and more colour to finally end up with pure black.

Fig 7.10
Courtesy of BMW Owners
Club (GB)

I have selected these ink
line and colour wash
drawings from an A2
size poster of a large range
of past models depicting
BMW's history.
I was given a selection of
photographs, those of which, in
my opinion, represented its history
best. When creating a montage such
as this, I always work size-for-size and place
all of the individual drawings on one sheet. These were
created on 'Daler' line and wash board NOT finish, as I
needed a surface to take both fine line ink drawings and
watercolour.
When creating montages of this nature, try to design an
interesting layout, in which all the disparate drawings
fit together.

such as Schmincke, Liquites, Lascaux and Gerstäcker offer a wide selection.

Within this chapter I give as many examples as possible of how to create images of cars using the mediums described. The mediums used are my choice; you might find others more to your liking, thus developing your own style and techniques.

Fig 7.11
Battle of the Titans
Watercolour
53 x 37cm /21 x 14½in

Any period from 1885 to the present day contains interesting subjects for pencil or brush as the constituents of motoring art are very diverse.

When the first Grand Prix took place in 1906, the cars that participated had an engine capacity of 18 litres, more than eight times the size of current Grand Prix Formula One cars. By 1914, engine capacity had been reduced to 4.5 litres.

For this painting of the 1914 French Grand Prix, I had to research the car and the location. The Circuit de Lyon was actually 12 miles south of the city of Lyon, near the towns of Givors, Rive de Gier and Mornant, and was set amongst rolling farmland dotted with poplar trees; typical central France, in fact. The time was early July, so it was hot and dusty, with the sun high in the summer sky.

The car is a 4.5 litre Mercedes-Benz with four-cylinders, 115bhp, driven by Christian Lautenschlager and Louis Wagner. This car still exists, so, after some research, I was able to find some good contemporary reference material and current photographs.

The Mercedes' main opponent in the 660 mile race was the Peugeot of George Boillo, with whom Lautenschlager had a race-long duel, but the Mercedes triumphed in the end with the Peugeot virtually falling apart on the last lap.

I always recommend with any drawing or painting that a great deal of time is spent on research before a single pencil line is drawn.

Figs 7.12 & 7.13

These two ink line drawings – a Stutz DV32 (fig 7.12, below) and a Packard (fig 7.13, left) – demonstrate how simple and effective line drawings can be.

For the Stutz drawing, I have deliberately not used any tone or block shading, just loose-style line work with detail and reflections drawn in a thinner line. The figures and the aircraft have been added to create period detail which makes for a more interesting composition. With the drawing of the Packard I have chosen a slightly different approach. The line work is much tighter with block shading for the areas under the wings and the wheel centres, and minimal dot shading used on the tyres to give them form.

An additional touch you may like to try on line drawings of this nature is to select a famous landmark from the car's country of origin; for the Packard I have chosen the American Presidents carved into Mount Rushmore, but the White House, Statue of Liberty, or even the Grand Canyon would have been just as acceptable.

Fig 7.14
Now for something completely different! Although this is another line drawing, it has been done in reverse for the purpose of creating a white on black background drawing.
This is achieved by leaving untouched those areas you want to see black, with white areas inked in. For this Alfa Romeo in the pits, its racing number 11 on the grille is inked black and the shadow under the car left blank on the original ink drawing. When scanned as a reverse drawing, the 11 became white; likewise, under the car showed up as black.
You can see the difference in the two drawings. It is a case of thinking through what the effects will be before starting work.

Fig 7.15
This group of line ink drawings shows another way to
create effective but relatively quick illustrations.
Using any reference that is convenient, pencil-in the
basic image. Then, with fine line marker pens, I use
Edding 01-03 pens, ink-in the outline.
If you wish to draw more than one image, to give a
pleasing flow and continuity to the overall illustration,
maintain the same basic direction of pen stroke, angled
either left, right, or even vertically (horizontally does not
seem to work) to achieve this.

Tony Gardiner

⑧ Motorsport – racing & rallying

The majority of people today, when they think of motoring art, automatically envisage artists drawing and painting motorsport. This was not always the case, and certainly not up until the late 1960s, as many contemporary artists portray everyday motoring scenes, both past and present.

Professional artists were either employed within the publicity and advertising studios of car manufacturers, or by agencies that had car companies as clients. Some of the more well-known artists of this period – Frank Wootton, Roy Nockolds, and Terrence Cuneo – were commissioned to paint pictures of new models. In this area, the artist's days were numbered because of 1) introduction of the Trade Descriptions Act,

(2) cost, and (3) time, all of which meant that photographs were more cost-effective. The images portrayed in brochures or adverts had to be true representations of the product as purchased; in the United Kingdom, artists often exaggerated car length to make them more appealing to the American market, as well as its own, which had to stop when the Trade Descriptions Act became law.

As motorsport became more popular with the ever-expanding motoring public, so, too, did art that depicted motor racing and rallying subjects. I was caught up in this phenomena to the extent that I avidly pored over motoring press reports of Grands Prix, the Monte Carlo Rally, or the Le Mans 24 Hour race to get inspiration for a new painting.

Motorsport has always given us heroes, all-time great drivers of decades past such as Juan Manuel Fangio, Stirling Moss and Jim Clark, and more recently Nigel Mansell and Michael

continued page 111

Sahara Challenge
Courtesy of Andrew Duerden

This half-tone sepia wash drawing depicts the Vauxhall 30/98 that took part in a Trans Sahara expedition during the 1930s.

105

Fig 8.1
Seapang Downpour – Reeves Artist Canvas Board
57 x 76cm/20 x 30in
Acrylics

'Seapang Downpour' came about as a result of Michael Schumacher retiring from Grand Prix racing. The inspiration was the 2001 Petronas Malaysian Grand Prix which was held at the Seapang Circuit, when a tropical rainstorm hit the circuit not long after the start of the race.

Fig 8.1/1a (ooposite bottom)
To create this composition (fig 8.1), I first drew the two Ferraris in normal perspective as one drawing side-by-side on Detail Paper, then reversed the drawing

and turned it upside-down in a photocopier (fig 8.1/1 opposite top). That is not the image you see in a reflection because that, too, is running in the same perspective plain as the actual cars. The only use for the upside-down image is for lining up vertically, you then create a true reflection in perspective – if you viewed it at eye level, it would appear to be flying over your head (fig 8.1/1a opposite). The combined image (fig 8.1/1) for both cars was then transferred onto a canvas board. I used Daler Rowney System 3 acrylic paints: Ultramarine mixed with Paynes Grey and a hint of Cadmium Red (hue) for the background, Vermillion (hue) for the Ferraris with Burnt Umber and Burnt Sienna to give tonal changes, and Titanium White for the highlights and reflections.

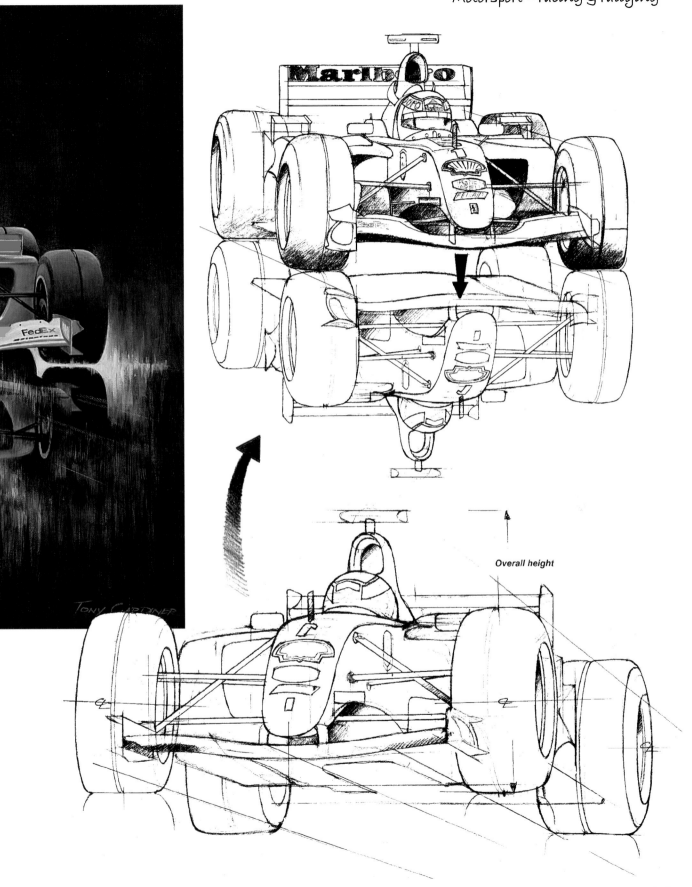

Overall height

Fig 8.2
Forest Racer
Courtesy of Andrew Duerden , Vauxhall Motorsport
Windsor & Newton, Artist Canvas Board
45.7 x 35.6cm/18 x 14in
Acrylics

For this particular painting, I wanted to create the effect of the dark forest as a backdrop with the car passing through a sunlit patch, enabling me to paint the 'Works' Vauxhall Astra in all its glory, in Red and White. Modern competition cars present the artist with different problems to, say, cars of the pre-1970s period, from when sponsors' logos and decals were the norm. The one thing you must be fully aware of is the car's body contours, where swage lines and curves are both concave and convex, plus the air ducts, skirts and air dams, because if there are spare surface areas, teams will sell it as advertising space.

This is where the artist has to be a bit of a signwriter because there is nothing worse than if all of these logos look as if they do not belong on a particular surface. One way to see how this works, although it might seem strange, is to pick a daily paper with a large typeface as a headline, mount it on a piece of thin card and then bend it, fold it, or even put a crease in it. Look at it from oblique angles and you will get an idea of how lettering appears on the various surfaces of a car.

The painting itself was fairly straightforward. I prepped the surface of the canvas board with extra coats of Gesso, as this particular canvas board was quite textured. Working with Daler Rowney System 3 acrylics, I used Ultramarine mixed with Paynes Grey and Phthalo Green, plus the odd dab of Burnt Sienna. The road surface was the same basic colours mixed with Titanium White. The car itself was a mix of Napthol Crimson and Cadmium Red to depict Vauxhall Red.

Fig 8.3
Storming the Futa Pass
Watercolour
47 x 35cm/19 x 14in

The Mercedes-Benz SSK has to be one of my all-time favourite sports cars, along with my love of long distance real road races and one of the great drivers, 'Rudolf Caracciola. The combination of all three gives you the perfect subject for a painting.

This is the 1931 Mille Miglia which was won at record speed by 'Rudi' Caracciola driving a highly-developed and very powerful version of the Mercedes-Benz SSK. He was the only German driver to ever win this famous Italian 1000 mile road race.

To attempt a subject such as this, the most important aspect, apart from your drawing and painting skills, is your research. There are examples of this car in the UK but this is where I suggest you acquire as many photographs, old motoring magazines and books as possible to create your own archive. Never throw anything away as it will be useful one day!

Schumacher – each generation has its very own hero.

Drawing and painting the race or rally car is no different to drawing or painting any other car subject, all you have to do is apply the skills and knowledge you have acquired as described throughout this book, especially in chapters 2 and 5. It is a matter of creating an interesting composition of a particular motorsport event, ensuring that components such as suspension, wheels and tyres are correctly drawn at the right angles, all other details are right for the model and year, and, last but not least, but most importantly, tonal recession of colour and perspective are accurate.

If all of these components come together there is no reason why you should not produce a very satisfactory and pleasing drawing or painting of Formula One, sports cars, saloons, or retro and historic racing cars. Single-seaters – Formula One

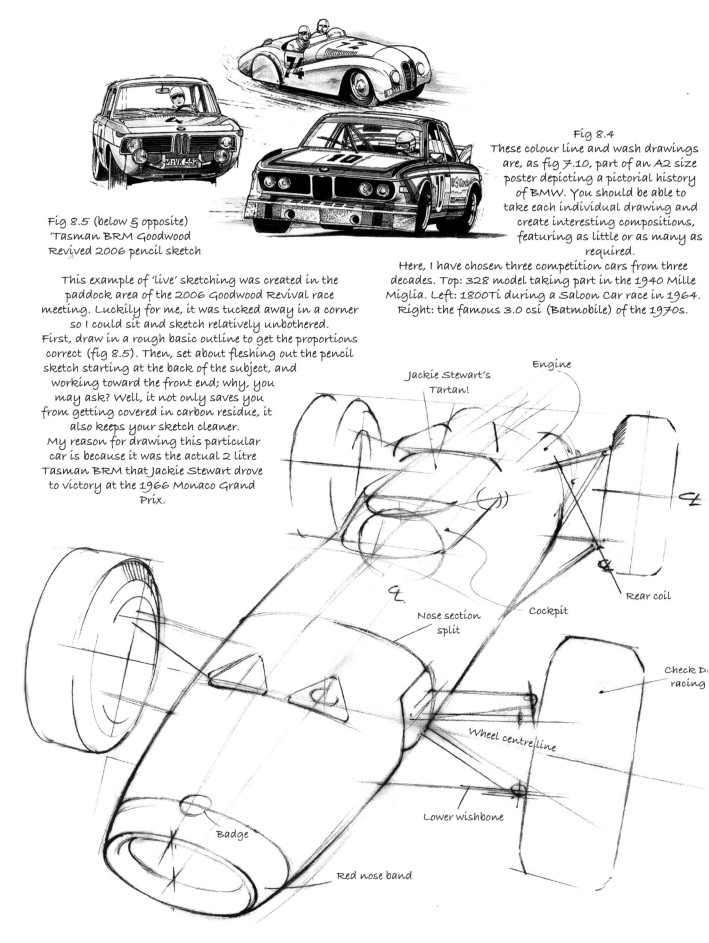

Fig 8.4
These colour line and wash drawings are, as fig 7.10, part of an A2 size poster depicting a pictorial history of BMW. You should be able to take each individual drawing and create interesting compositions, featuring as little or as many as required.

Here, I have chosen three competition cars from three decades. Top: 328 model taking part in the 1940 Mille Miglia. Left: 1800Ti during a Saloon Car race in 1964. Right: the famous 3.0 csi (Batmobile) of the 1970s.

Fig 8.5 (below & opposite)
'Tasman BRM Goodwood Revived 2006 pencil sketch

This example of 'live' sketching was created in the paddock area of the 2006 Goodwood Revival race meeting. Luckily for me, it was tucked away in a corner so I could sit and sketch relatively unbothered.
First, draw in a rough basic outline to get the proportions correct (fig 8.5). Then, set about fleshing out the pencil sketch starting at the back of the subject, and working toward the front end; why, you may ask? Well, it not only saves you from getting covered in carbon residue, it also keeps your sketch cleaner.
My reason for drawing this particular car is because it was the actual 2 litre Tasman BRM that Jackie Stewart drove to victory at the 1966 Monaco Grand Prix.

Jackie Stewart's Tartan!

Engine

Rear coil

Nose section split

Cockpit

Check D racing

Wheel centre line

Lower wishbone

Badge

Red nose band

Goodwood revival 2006

cars – are no more difficult to paint or draw than any other car, though do demand more attention to detail because major components such as tyres, wheels and engines are more visible than on sports or saloon cars, and there are drivers and sponsor colour schemes to take into account.

Prior to the late 1960s, advertising logos were only seen on competition cars in America and Australia, as advertising was banned in the United Kingdom and Europe. In 1969 Lotus was one of the first racing teams to run its cars in sponsor colours, that of the tobacco company, John Player, running as Gold Leaf Team Lotus, Gold Leaf being a brand of cigarette. All Lotus cars were painted with the red, white and gold colour scheme instead of the traditional British Racing Green. From that

moment on, virtually no racing car carried its country's national colours, although there were exceptions: Ferrari cars have never been painted in anything other than Italian Racing Red, and some French teams always use French Blue as the base colour of their schemes. To a certain extent the artist found he needed signwriter skills to paint miniature sponsor logos and decals on bodywork, which, by the mid-1970s, was also changing: gone was the smooth, cigar-shaped bodywork of Formula One cars, replaced by the wedge shape, complete with wings, skirts and other aerodynamic aids.

I make no apology for this section on motor

continued page 117

Fig 8.6
1966 Monaco Grand Prix
watercolour
51 x 38cm/20x 15in

Once again I was attracted to creating a painting of my
favourite race circuit because it is the last remaining
street circuit in use today. This time I have chosen to
depict what was then known as Station's Hairpin,
although today the station is long gone, but in 1966 it
was still there. This point on the circuit was one of the
slowest corners and the most interesting.
Although for the finished painting I chose a completely
different viewpoint to my sketch, it was good reference
for the cockpit and suspension detail. To create the sunlit
street of Monte Carlo, apart from the dark green of the
BRM, the colours were basically the same as in fig 5.1.
The Ferrari of John Surtees, Vermillion (hue) was used
but washed down. I used Ultramarine Blue on the car's
upper surfaces for the sky reflections.

Fig 8.7
VX Racing Vauxhall Vectra – BTCC Brands Hatch
Bockingford 425gm watercolour paper
33 x 46cm/13 x 18in
Courtesy of Andrew Duerden (Vauxhall Motorsport)

This painting shows clearly the problem artists have depicting current race and rally cars with their complicated colour schemes and graphics, so you have to be very aware of surface changes. These colour schemes present the artist with a different challenge of creating a decal-free, highly-polished painted surface.
I wanted to make the Vectra stand out, so, to the pursuing Honda glued to the Vectra's boot, I applied only a very light colour wash to emphasize the Vauxhall's prominence. Likewise, I felt it unnecessary to create any background other than with colour over-sprayed with a paint diffuser.

Fig 8.8
The Thin Green Line
Bockingford 300gm watercolour paper
43 x 53cm/17 x 21in

The Vanwall was another of those cars whose Grand Prix success when driven by the likes of Stirling Moss, Tony Brookes and American, Harry Schell, was the inspiration for my lifelong love affair with drawing and painting the motocar.

I was actually researching another painting through old motoring magazines when I found a photo of the start of the 1957 Italian Grand Prix at Monza, Italy. This brings me to another aspect of drawing and painting the car – reference material – which doesn't appear overnight. I have built up a library of motoring books and magazines, plus thousands of photographs taken by myself and those of motor manufacturers. Companies such as Ford and Vauxhall still have their own photo archives which supply photos free of charge, but the rest of the British Car Industry's archives are deposited at the British Heritage Museum at Gaydon, Warwickshire, or the National Motor Museum at Bealieu, Hampshire, both of which charge for prints.

My suggestion is to visit auto jumbles and car boot sales, and acquire any material you might find useful for future reference.

Fig 8.9 (opposite)
Monte Carlo or Bust
Bristol Board, line ink drawing
28 x 18cm/11 x 17in

Sometimes, a stylised approach is required for an ink drawing of this nature. I have employed all of the known techniques used by illustrators to create surfaces or light and shade; i.e. line, dot and cross hatching.

Although this is hand-drawn and not a pure technical illustration as such, basic drawing aids, like a rule and french curves, were used. For the background I decided to use vertical lines to show the shaded areas, and for the snow I used the dot technique (this can take a lot of time to complete).

For the car, a 1932 MGJ2, I used all the textures: lines for the bodywork, cross hatching for the roof fabric and the grille, and dots representing tyre rubber, but much denser than on the snow.

Like the Mini Cooper 'S' (Fig 7.5), if an illustration was needed in the 1950s for an advertisement in the press, the artist would use a technique such as this because it would reproduce as a cleaner, crisper image than some other photo images of that period, due to the poor quality of newsprint which would absorb the ink off the presses and give a poor, blotchy image.

racing; my interest lies in the golden era of motoring and motor racing that spanned the period 1920-1970, when old established marques such as Bentley, Mercedes-Benz, Bugatti, Alfa Romeo and Maserati battled it out on Europe's motor racing circuits. After World War II came the new upstarts to take up the challenge. From the United Kingdom it was Jaguar, Vanwall, Connaught, Lotus, Cooper and BRM, along with a mighty onslaught backed by millions of US dollars spent by Ford of America to create the famous Ford GT40 in the late 1960s, in order to combat Ferrari's domination of sports car racing.

This was the period that had the most influence on my work as an artist, the Jaguar D Type generating this lifelong passion for drawing and painting motorcars.

From the very beginning of motorsport and the great inter-city road races of a hundred years ago, to the current contrived – and somewhat clinical – racing circuits of today, artists have portrayed many of the epic duels when man and machine have been pitted against other competitors, and, as long as motorsports exists, artists will continue to do so.

Fig 8.10
The Victor's Departure
Watercolour
47.5 x 37.5cm/19 x 15in

Throughout the history of the motorcar, certain
manufacturers have always been at the fore in
various forms of motorsport – hence the plethora of
paintings within this publication depicting the cars of
Mercedes-Benz.
This watercolour shows the winning Mercedes 220SE
saloon, driven by Walter Shock/Rolf Moll, about to leave
the St Claude time control in central France during the
1960 Monte Carlo Rally.
During my travels in recent years, I have taken
photographs of such venues for my archive. You never
know when they might be just the material you require
for background reference.

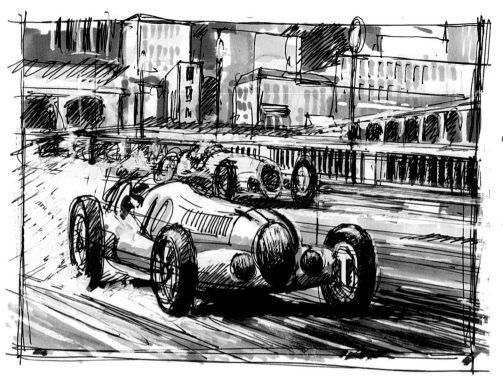

Fig 8.11/1
Shown here is my very first
thoughts for this painting,
drawn on a piece of 6 x
4½in/15 x 11cm scrap paper,
using a fine line ballpoint pen,
marker pens and correction
fluid.
If an idea comes to you at any
time, get your thoughts onto
paper as quickly as possible,
then develop the idea when you
have more time, eventually
creating the final image.

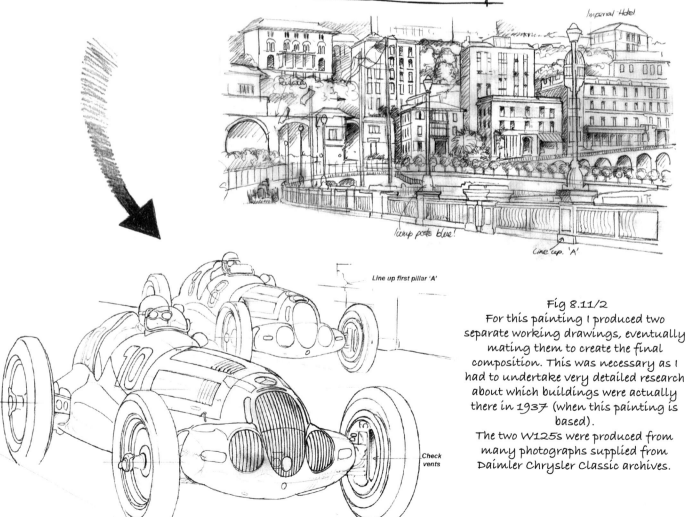

Imperial Hotel

'camp posts blue!'

Line up 'A'

Line up first pillar 'A'

Check
vents

Fig 8.11/2
For this painting I produced two
separate working drawings, eventually
mating them to create the final
composition. This was necessary as I
had to undertake very detailed research
about which buildings were actually
there in 1937 (when this painting is
based).
The two W125s were produced from
many photographs supplied from
Daimler Chrysler Classic archives.

Fig 8.11/3
1937 Monaco Grand Prix – Watercolour
53.7 x 37.5cm/21 x 14½in

For this particular painting, I decided to create a view looking back at the famous waterfront as the cars race along it. If you stood on the same spot today, fewer than six of the buildings from 1937 remain.

The first thumbnail sketch (see Fig 8.11/1 opposite, top) was created virtually as a doodle using fine line pens, plus markers in cool and warm greys.

During my visits in recent years, I have taken photos to use as reference material to check on colour and period architectural accuracy. To create the two W125 Mercedes Benz GP cars, photo references from Mercedes Benz' own museum in Stuttgart were used. Eventually, I mated together the two pencil sketches of the background and cars. (See fig 8.11/2 opposite.)

The architecture of Monte Carlo is essentially light beige with Terra Cotta, Yellow Ochre and all shades in-between. Likewise, the paving on the harbour front that the cars were racing along is a sandy beige colour. For the background, I laid on a basic light wash of Burnt Sienna and Yellow Ochre mix, working in various shades of the two colours.

The cars themselves were, of course, silver, so I left the basic white of the paper with a wash of Ultramarine Blue on the top surface; Paynes Grey was added for the lower body sides with background colour. For the shadows, I never use black, but a mix of Sepia and Phaleo Blue, with odd dashes of Burnt Sienna, finished off with flicks of Permanent White to add movement.

One trick I use is to paint the portion of the car nearest (this could apply to a rear view) in a deeper, crisp colour, whilst fading away in colour depth the furthest portion; this helps give the illusion of speed and movement.

We hope that this book has provided some insight to
the world of drawing and painting cars, whether you are
interested just for your own pleasure or more commercial
reasons. Unfortunately, it is not a world of champagne and
roses; at times, it is a hard slog along a long and winding
road.
The satisfaction comes from producing images of one of the
most exciting and, at times, controversial means of transport
devised by mankind. Whatever happens in the future, the
car will be with us for a long time yet, and with it artists who
capture it in paintings and drawings using a variety of media.

RAC Rally Action!

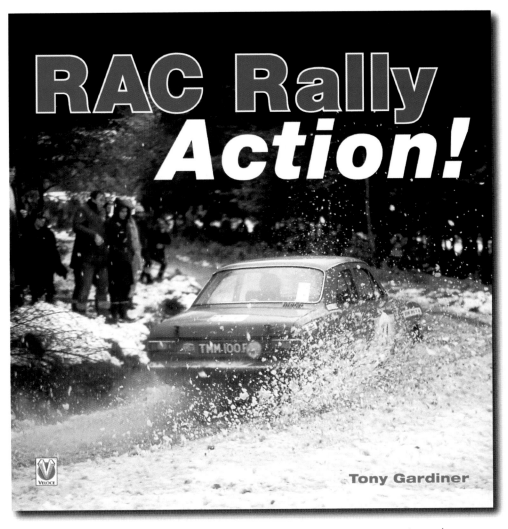

£35.99* • Hardback • 250mm x 250mm • 208 pages • 330 colour & b&w pictures
ISBN 978-1-903706-97-8 • UPC 6-36847-00297-8

This book covers the pre-WRC golden years: the Rally of the Forests period. With access to crew notes & manufacturers' archives, & containing many previously unpublished pictures, the history and excitement of the RAC International Rally of Great Britain has been captured forever in Tony Gardiner's book.

* Prices subject to change. p+p extra. for more details visit www.veloce.co.uk or email info@veloce.co.uk.

1½-litre Grand Prix Racing 1961-65

£39.99* • Hardback • 250mm x 250mm • 336 pages • 204 b&w pictures
ISBN 978-1-84584-016-7 • UPC 6-36847-04016-1

The story of a Grand Prix formula that no British constructor wanted but which they came to almost totally dominate. It saw the career of Stirling Moss come to a premature end, and in his absence the rise to prominence of a new breed of British driver in Jim Clark, Graham Hill and John Surtees.

* *Prices subject to change. p+p extra. for more details visit www.veloce.co.uk or email info@veloce.co.uk.*

PEKING TO PARIS

THE ULTIMATE DRIVING ADVENTURE

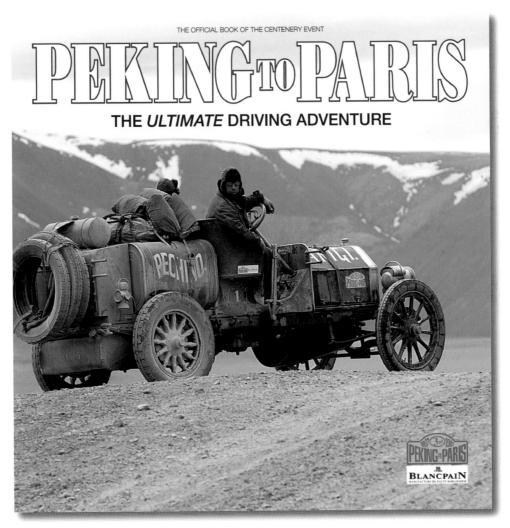

£29.99* • Hardback • 250mm x 250mm • 224 pages • 456 colour & b&w pictures
ISBN 978-1-84584-120-1 • UPC 6-36847-04120-5

Vivid daily diary of the 40-day drive from Peking to Paris. 130 intrepid drivers, in cars ranging from a 1903 Mercedes eight-litre and original 'Great Race' Itala, to a 1967 Aston Martin, race through the Gobi Desert, Outer Mongolia, and across Russia to Europe ...

* Prices subject to change. p+p extra. for more details visit www.veloce.co.uk or email info@veloce.co.uk.

A DRIVE ON THE
Wild SIDE

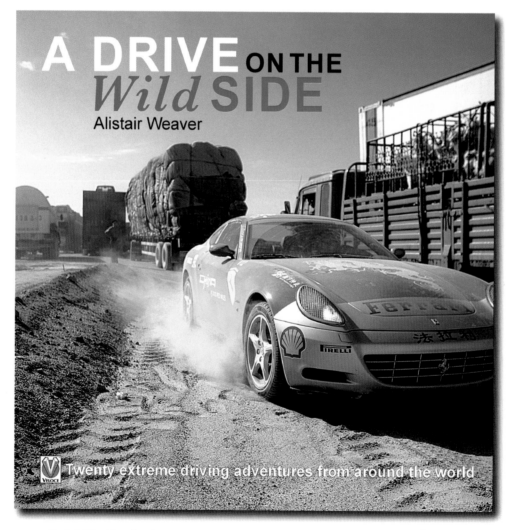

£29.99* • Hardback • 250mm x 250mm • 176 pages • 341 colour pictures
ISBN 978-1-84584-100-3 • UPC 6-36847-04100-7

Experience and relish electrifying journeys along some of the world's most exciting roads. Thoroughly researched, beautifully written, and illustrated by some of the world's leading automotive and travel photographers, here are the fascinating, hair-raising and moving accounts of some stunning automotive adventures.

* Prices subject to change. p+p extra. for more details visit www.veloce.co.uk or email info@veloce.co.uk.

Index